IoT Standards with Blockchain

Enterprise Methodology for Internet of Things

Venkatesh Upadrista

Apress®

IoT Standards with Blockchain: Enterprise Methodology for Internet of Things

Venkatesh Upadrista
Slough, UK

ISBN-13 (pbk): 978-1-4842-7270-1   ISBN-13 (electronic): 978-1-4842-7271-8
https://doi.org/10.1007/978-1-4842-7271-8

Managing Director, Apress Media LLC: Welmoed Spahr
Acquisitions Editor: Aaron Black
Development Editor: James Markham
Coordinating Editor: Jessica Vakili

Distributed to the book trade worldwide by Springer Science+Business Media New York, 1 NY Plaza, New York, NY 10014. Phone 1-800-SPRINGER, fax (201) 348-4505, e-mail orders-ny@springer-sbm.com, or visit www.springeronline.com. Apress Media, LLC is a California LLC and the sole member (owner) is Springer Science + Business Media Finance Inc (SSBM Finance Inc). SSBM Finance Inc is a **Delaware** corporation.

For information on translations, please e-mail booktranslations@springernature.com; for reprint, paperback, or audio rights, please e-mail bookpermissions@springernature.com.

Apress titles may be purchased in bulk for academic, corporate, or promotional use. eBook versions and licenses are also available for most titles. For more information, reference our Print and eBook Bulk Sales web page at http://www.apress.com/bulk-sales.

Any source code or other supplementary material referenced by the author in this book is available to readers on GitHub via the book's product page, located at www.apress.com/978-1-4842-7270-1. For more detailed information, please visit http://www.apress.com/source-code.

Printed on acid-free paper

Table of Contents

iii

About the Author

Venkatesh Upadrista specializes in driving growth for digital and analytics business and is currently working as a delivery leader for UKI portfolio for a large IT services company. He has been a guest lecturer at Rutgers Business School (USA) and board member to several start-ups in the past. He is currently on the board of Futurelight Technologies acting as their Digital Advisor. Futurelight Technologies is a digital services and products company which operates with design thinking to deliver a portfolio of next-generation products and services with a blend of deep domain expertise in Internet of Things and Artificial Intelligence. Apart from his professional achievements, Mr. Upadrista has so far authored six books on topics ranging from business lead digital transformation, Agile, cloud, Internet of Things, and vendor management. He is recognized as an exceptional digital talent leader by UK Tech Nation and speaks at industry conferences on digital transformation topics covering Agile, cloud, data analytics, and Internet of Things.

About the Technical Reviewer

 **Massimo Nardone** has more than 22 years of experience in security, web/mobile development, cloud, and IT architecture. His truc IT passions arc security and Android.

He has been programming and teaching how to program with Android, Perl, PHP, Java, VB, Python, C/C++, and MySQL for more than 20 years.

He holds a master of science degree in computing science from the University of Salerno, Italy.

He has worked as a project manager, software engineer, research engineer, chief security architect, information security manager, PCI/SCADA auditor, and senior lead IT security/cloud/SCADA architect for many years.

Introduction

Digital transformation is the transformation of business and organizational activities, processes, competencies, and models to fully leverage the opportunities of a mix of digital technologies and their accelerating impact across industries in a strategic and prioritized way, with present and future shifts in mind.

Digital transformation is not about technology, but it is a way for enterprises to do business and operations differently to remain competitive and be disruptive in their marketspace. To achieve this change, technology is utilized. Being digital requires enterprises to be open to reexamining their entire way of doing business and understanding where the new frontiers of value are and how technology can play a key role in bringing this value faster. In practice, end-to-end customer experience optimization, operational flexibility, and innovation are key drivers and goals of digital transformation, along with the development of new revenue sources and information-powered ecosystems of value, leading to business transformation and new forms of digital processes.

The Internet of Things (IoT) is one of the most widely spoken digital technologies that promises a lot of benefits to enterprises. IoT is all about connecting devices and factory equipment over the Internet. In other words, it is the convergence between Operational Technology (OT) and Information Technology (IT).

OT is about (heavy) machineries, safety of people, and so on. There is almost zero tolerance toward downtime, errors, and safety. This is one of the core reasons why OT has always operated in a highly risk-averse manner. Another aspect of OT is that the machineries deployed at the factories cannot be upgraded or replaced at the same pace as IT systems, and these are the ones that will remain for years once purchased. This becomes a hurdle to deploy new innovative ideas on these machineries to make them more efficient. From a people perspective, these two departments (IT and OT) have traditionally and culturally not spent a lot of time together. A typical IT department is measured on system uptime, availability of applications and IT infrastructure, number of security breaches, and reducing costs of IT. On the other hand, the OT department constitutes of the factory managers, production managers, and even agriculture farmers. These are the folks who produce food, control the oil and gas process, or pump oil from the ground. An OT department is measured on entirely different success criteria, such as what is the yield of the crop, how much water is being used to create that yield, what is the production uptime of the factory, and so on.

IT and OT departments are two different worlds, and each department is measured very different on success. With IoT, both these departments need to come together, and this is where connecting people becomes equally important along with connecting things. Successful IoT use cases have provided several benefits to enterprises such as opening up new business opportunities and increased revenue along with powering enterprises with an ability to perform better operations and become more productive, more protected, and more profitable. A classic example is the smart fridge. Using IoT, a fridge could tell us it was out of milk, text us if its internal camera saw there was no milk left, or that the carton was past its expiry date. The benefits of IoT to enterprises are enormous if applied carefully, and this is one of the reasons why IoT has become so popular. However, IoT is in a very early stage of maturity, and several guidelines and ways of working are still being defined to bring standardization in IoT projects.

Though IoT is a relatively new area for many enterprises, this cannot stop us on our journey toward excellence with IoT. The good news is that there are several guidelines, mature practices, tools, and technologies that have already been developed, and by carefully choosing the right ones, enterprises can achieve success with IoT. This book is one such step toward standardizing an end-to-end IoT implementation approach and is based on several best practices and successes in IoT that have been achieved in the past across multiple industries.

This book defines an enterprise digital transformation framework for IoT, called IoT Standards, that will enable enterprises to do business better and achieve operational benefits using IoT.

This book is intended for all chief executives, technology leaders, and business leaders who intend to successfully embark on an IoT-led digital transformation journey with business as the core driver for the transformation for their enterprise.

This book is an outcome of multiple successful engagements in IoT which I have led during the last several years. Finally, this book is also an outcome of my learnings and those of my colleagues on failed IoT projects – a combination which had helped me to define a solid methodology to execute large-scale enterprise-level IoT use case implementation.

Before officially releasing this methodology into the market, IoT Standards were implemented at several organizations. The methodology has demonstrated superior benefits when compared to any other guidance available in the industry today. There are several case studies described in the book, all of which are from experiences with real companies, but their names have been changed to disguise their identity.

PART I

IoT Business Strategy

This part provides a perspective on the importance of digital transformation using IoT for enterprises, along with the successes and failures many enterprises have achieved from digital transformation in the last few years.

We will also discuss about the business strategies for enterprises to adopt and remain relevant in the marketspace based on which the digital transformation road map using IoT can be defined.

CHAPTER 1

Getting Started

Technology has been in existence for many years, and over the course of time, new age technologies have completely revolutionized the IT industry.

The modern age is referred to as the "digital age" since more and more technologies are stacking onto each other and developing into something greater. Consumers and businesses alike are expecting to see more opportunities for growth as future technology develops further.

For some enterprises, being digital is solely concerned with technology. For others, being digital is a new way of engaging with customers, whereas for a small minority it represents an entirely new way of doing business. Although all these definitions of digital are correct in their own sense, often such diverse perspectives trip up leadership teams since they reflect a lack of alignment and common vision regarding the direction their business needs to go. This often results in piecemeal initiatives or misguided efforts that lead to missed opportunities, lackluster performance, or even false starts.

Enterprises and business executives need to have a clear and common understanding of exactly what digital means to them and what they want to achieve. As a result of this, they need to understand what it means to their business based upon which digital strategies or digital transformation initiatives should be defined to drive business performance. Digital transformation is all about doing business better or bringing efficiencies in their operating model using modern technologies.

© Venkatesh Upadrista 2021
V. Upadrista, *IoT Standards with Blockchain*,
https://doi.org/10.1007/978-1-4842-7271-8_1

Although digital is becoming mainstream for many enterprises, it is essential to understand that for many enterprises legacy is going to remain and cannot be completely eliminated. Digital is all about using modern technologies (also called as digital technologies) and integrating it with legacy to make modern and legacy work together coherently to deliver business results. As an example, legacy machinery are there to live in the factories for the next several decades, and using digital technology, enterprises should be able to bring value by applying modern technologies alongside these legacy machinery with minimal changes.

Being digital requires enterprises to be open to reexamining their entire way of doing business and understanding where the new frontiers of value are and how technology can play a key role in showcasing this value faster.

Digital for enterprises is all about rethinking how to use new capabilities, tools, and technologies to improve how customers are served while at the same time reducing IT costs and overall working more efficiently.

To understand how to better serve the customers as an example, one needs to understand each step of a customer's purchasing journey – regardless of channel – and think about how digital capabilities can design and deliver the best possible experience, across all parts of the business. For example, the supply chain is critical to developing the flexibility, efficiency, and speed to deliver the right product in a way the customer wants. By the same token, data and metrics can focus on delivering insights about customers that in turn drive marketing and sales decisions.

To improve efficiency, enterprises can use digital technologies to understand their current operations and bring in automation. As an example, real-time monitoring of energy using the Internet of Things allows manufacturers to detect off-hours consumption, optimize manufacturing production schedules, identify anomalies, and capitalize on opportunities for savings. In another example, by benchmarking similar pieces of equipment or comparable locations, manufacturers uncover systems that are not functioning properly to detect hidden operational inefficiencies and energy waste.

On reducing the cost of IT, enterprises need to understand how the existing IT landscape stacks up on value vs. cost and what drivers in the market exist that can reduce their CAPEX and OPEX costs, with cloud, for example, being the biggest opportunity to do just this. Aside from cost reduction, automation plays a pivotal role in ensuring that operational efficiencies are improving over a period of time. As more and more automation is enabled (be it in customer journeys, business process flow automation, operations, or development), enterprises will see increased efficiency in their business and reduction of the total cost of ownership. There will be lesser defects due to human errors, and enterprises will move away from active monitoring to active auditing. Ultimately, this means there will be less efforts spent in day-to-day monitoring of services by humans, and to ensure things are going right, more time will be spent in auditing.

Definitions

Active monitoring *means that there is a full-time team who continuously monitors for errors. In contrast to active monitoring,* **active auditing** *means that checks are performed at certain predefined intervals for errors. Active auditing does not need a dedicated team since most of the checks are automated and performed by machines. If an error is identified, resolution is automated so that the same error does not occur in future.*

Development *is the process of creating a new software or product or an infrastructure. This goes through a process of planning, creating, testing, and deploying an information system.*

Maintenance or *Operations* is the process of maintaining the developed software or product or infrastructure. Operations is not just about fixing defects but modifying a software product or an infrastructure after delivery to correct faults, as well as to improve performance. Small enhancements are also performed as part of operations.

Digital is not about delivering a one-off customer journey or a one-off improvement in total cost of ownership. It is about continuous improvements where processes and capabilities are constantly evolving based on inputs from the industry or the customer. This fosters ongoing product or service loyalty, and to enable this, enterprises need to create the right digital foundation that will allow the organization to achieve their business goals.

Digital foundation is all about utilizing technology and organizational processes that allow an enterprise to do their business with full agility.

Designing Business for Future

There are four pillars that are critical to guide organizations' thinking when they are assessing strategies for business transformation. These can be found in the following:

- The right business model – Becoming digital is not simply about taking existing products or customer interactions and experiences and putting them online. Enduring success in the digital economy means fundamentally rethinking how business is conducted today. The way in which organizations get products to market through centralized catalogues and move to deliver entirely new consumption models (such as pervasive digital services and subscriptions rather than one-off purchases) in addition to how consumers now purchase and use offerings is fundamental.

- The right partners – Businesses that work together with digital partners across industry borders achieve far beyond what any individual business could do on its own in the ever-changing digital world. To achieve this, businesses must now integrate with a myriad of existing and third-party systems, streamline and simplify business processes, and develop efficient improvements that decrease operational risks and expenses. The sharing of knowledge and unique experiences to develop new applications, products, and services will become essential.

- The right technology – Not all platforms are created equal, and that will become painfully evident to those that do not choose wisely and bravely. The cost of legacy system infrastructure maintenance, integration, and operations will become prohibitive when digital competitors operate at a fraction of the cost. Not all legacy can be replaced however, and there is a right balance to be made between legacy and digital for every enterprise.

- The right mindset – Providing evolved customer experiences regardless of who those customers are, from consumers to vendors to partners, is vital to digital success, but it is only half the equation. To survive and (most importantly) flourish, a digital culture must be integrated at all levels of the organization to instill the mentality of agility and continuous learning the digital economy demands. This requires a change to the enterprise workforce and operating model.

There is no one-size-fits-all approach to digital transformation; each strategy will be unique to each organization. However, a focus on balancing activities across these four pillars provides the compass to guide a successful transformation.

The Internet of Things As a Digital Enabler

The Internet of Things (IoT) is one of the most widely spoken digital technologies that promises a lot of value to enterprises. IoT is all about connecting devices over the Internet, allowing them to talk to each other and many different systems, applications, and so on. A classic example is the smart fridge. Using IoT, a fridge could tell us it was out of milk, text us if its internal camera saw there was no milk left, or that the carton was past its expiry date. All this is possible with IoT, and this is one of the reasons why IoT is becoming so popular. When we talk about IoT, it is a combination of both hardware and software talking to one another.

The hardware utilized in IoT systems includes devices for a remote dashboard, devices for control, servers, a routing device, and sensors. These devices manage key tasks and functions such as system activation, action specifications, security, communication, and detection to support specific goals and actions.

The software used in IoT includes systems that collect data from the hardware devices. IoT software addresses key areas of networking and action through platforms, embedded systems, and middleware. These individual applications are responsible for data collection, device integration, real-time analytics, and application and process extension within the IoT network. They exploit integration with critical business systems (e.g., ordering systems) in the execution of related tasks. These terms will be explained further later.

IIoT (Industrial IoT) and IoMT (Internet of Medical Things) are other most widely used phrases in the IoT world. IIoT is the current trend of automation and data exchange in manufacturing technologies. It includes cyber-physical systems, the Internet of Things, and cloud computing. Industry 4.0 creates what has been called a "smart factory." IoMT is all about the Internet of Medical Things. The IoMT is a connected infrastructure of medical devices, software applications, and health systems and services.

Whether we talk about IIoT or IoMT, integrating IT systems with operational technologies always comes first. In short, this is called IT-OT integration.

Gartner, Inc. forecasted that the enterprise and automotive IoT market[1] will grow to 5.8 billion endpoints in 2020, a 21% increase from 2019. By the end of 2019, 4.8 billion endpoints were expected to be in use, up 21.5% from 2018. An endpoint, from an IoT perspective, is a physical computing device that performs a function or task as part of an Internet-connected product or service. An endpoint, for example, could be a wearable fitness device, an industrial control system, an automotive telematics unit, or even a personal drone unit.

Utilities will be the highest user of IoT endpoints, which have totaled 1.17 billion endpoints in 2019 and have increased 17% in 2020 reaching 1.37 billion endpoints. Electricity smart metering, both residential and commercial, will boost the adoption of IoT among utilities is the prediction. Physical security, where building intruder detection and indoor surveillance use cases will drive volume, will be the second largest IoT use case in 2020.[2]

---

[1] www.gartner.com/en/newsroom/press-releases/2019-08-29-gartner-says-5-8-billion-enterprise-and-automotive-io#:~:text=Gartner%2C%20Inc.,a%2021%25%20increase%20from%202019.&text=Utilities%20will%20be%20the%20highest,to%20reach%201.37%20billion%20endpoints

[2] www.gartner.com/en/newsroom/press-releases/2019-08-29-gartner-says-5-8-billion-enterprise-and-automotive-io

The four core elements that make up an IoT ecosystem are depicted in Figure 1-1.

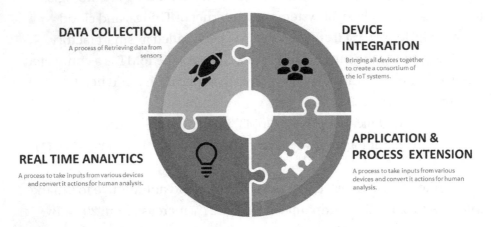

DATA COLLECTION
A process of Retrieving data from sensors

DEVICE INTEGRATION
Bringing all devices together to create a consortium of the IoT systems.

REAL TIME ANALYTICS
A process to take inputs from various devices and convert it actions for human analysis.

APPLICATION & PROCESS EXTENSION
A process to take inputs from various devices and convert it actions for human analysis.

Figure 1-1. *Four core elements in an IoT ecosystem*

Data collection – This is the process of retrieving data from sources such as sensors. It uses certain protocols to aid sensors in connecting with real-time, machine-to-machine networks. It then collects data from multiple devices and distributes it in accordance with settings. It also works in reverse by distributing data over devices, and the system eventually transmits all collected data to a central server.

Device integration – Device integration software brings all the devices together to create a consortium of the IoT systems. It ensures the necessary cooperation and stable networking between devices.

Real-time analytics – These applications take data or input from various devices and convert it into viable actions or clear patterns for human analysis. They analyze information based on various settings and designs, after which certain actions are taken either manually or automatically.

Application and process extension – Applications extend the reach of existing systems and software to allow a wider, more effective system. They integrate predefined devices for specific purposes such as allowing certain mobile devices or engineering instruments access. It supports improved productivity and more accurate data collection.

From the preceding discussion, it is clear that IoT is not just about devices. It is an integration between Information Technology and Operational Technology.

Definition

Shop floor *is the area of a factory, machine shop, etc. where people work on machines, or the space in a retail establishment where goods are sold to consumers.*

Operational Technology (OT) is about managing, monitoring, and controlling industrial operations with a focus on the physical devices and processes used in the shop floor where the production of goods takes place.

IT includes the use of computers, storage, networking devices, other physical devices and infrastructure, as well as processes to create, process, store, secure, and exchange all forms of electronic data.

Operational Technology – A Preview

OT is about (heavy) machineries, safety of people, and so on. There is almost zero tolerance toward downtime, errors, and safety. This is one of the core reasons why OT has always operated in a highly risk-averse manner. Another aspect of OT is that the machineries deployed at the factories cannot be upgraded or replaced at the same pace as IT systems, and these are the ones that will remain for years once purchased. This becomes a hurdle to deploy new innovative ideas on these machineries to make them more efficient. On the other hand, most of the machineries operate 24/7 and 365 days a year, and stopping these machineries for any desired upgrades or modification is an almost impossible task.

In the consumer-facing OT world in the last few years, there have been tremendous advancements made. As an example, in the older days we were carrying analogue phones, and now almost everybody uses a smartphone. We were also previously driving manual cars although many of us have now made the switch to electric or automatic.

The nonconsumer-facing OT world however has not changed at all – in the mining industry, for example, several decades ago hammers, chisels, pickaxes, and shovels were being used, and still are to this day. Similarly, in the manufacturing industry years back, they were using conveyor belts, painting robots, welding robots, and so on. Fast forward to today, and we have the same equipment. The three key reasons why changes have not occurred is because

- Safety – Safety is to prevent or lessen the risk of workplace injury, illness, and death and therefore is of paramount importance in the OT world. Safety is keeping people away from physical harm, and there is zero tolerance toward safety compromises.

- Reliability – Reliability is defined as the probability that a component (or an entire system) will perform its function for a specified period of time, when operating in its design environment.

- Cost and risk to change or upgrades – The cost of change to machinery is quite high, and with almost zero downtime expected on machineries, upgrades are also hard to manage. Secondly, an error from upgrading can lead to reliability issues. This is one of the reasons why in the OT world there is a tendency to avoid quick patches, software updates, etc., because they may result in safety or reliability concerns.

There are several challenges in making changes to the OT systems, such as manufacturing or mining equipment. However, with more and more benefits that enterprises are gaining because of IoT, they have the desire to change, but an uncompromised requirement is safety and security. A poorly planned change (even as simple as an antivirus update) can introduce enough risk of disruption to an industrial network that OT experts are scared about as people's lives may be at risk because of a badly managed change.

IT/OT convergence or IT-OT integration is the integration of Information Technology (IT) systems with Operational Technology (OT) systems. IT systems are used for data-centric computing; OT systems monitor events, processes, and devices and make adjustments in enterprise and industrial operations.

The main difference between OT and IT devices is that OT devices control the physical world, while IT systems manage data.

The IT team is the Information Technology team and constitutes of roles such as data analysts, data scientists, developers, and testers. An OT team could be factory managers, production managers, and even agriculture farmers. These are the folks who produce food, control the oil and gas process, pump oil from the ground, or who are responsible for maintaining the fleet of company trucks.

In the long term, not making necessary changes, such as upgrading, and not adopting to IoT may lead to an increased risk of a deliberate disruption by a hacker. A well-known example of such a disruption was the Stuxnet attack in Iran. In January 2010, inspectors with the International Atomic Energy Agency visiting the Natanz uranium enrichment plant in Iran noticed that filters used to enrich uranium gas were failing at an unprecedented rate. The cause was a complete mystery, and Iranian technicians replaced the filters. Five months later, a seemingly unrelated event occurred. A computer security firm in Belarus was called in to troubleshoot a series of computers in Iran that were crashing and rebooting repeatedly. The researchers found a handful of malicious files on one of the systems and discovered the Stuxnet virus. Another more recent event occurred last year in Germany, where hackers used malware to gain access to the control system of a steel mill, which they disrupted to such a degree that it could not be shut down. Thankfully, there was no damage to human life. These two examples highlight that OT systems are not fully secured and need to be upgraded at regular intervals. On the other side, IT-OT integration is mandatory for all enterprises that wish to be relevant in the market.

The IT-OT Integration

Until today, OT has very limited integration with the IT. The reason behind this is that OT is all about machinery, safety of people, and the creation of products. Today, more and more organizations are embracing IoT technologies such as smart meters and self-monitoring transformers. We are also seeing production lines and farm equipment outfitted with sensors.

The rise of these new technologies has created a need for organizations to optimize how machines, applications, and infrastructure collect, transmit, and process data. Done right, IT-OT convergence gives businesses the ability to fix critical issues faster, make informed business decisions, and scale processes across both physical and virtual systems. Figure 1-2 depicts a simple block diagram on how an IoT ecosystem works.

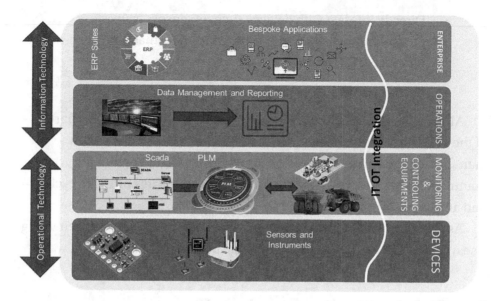

Figure 1-2. *IT-OT integration reference diagram*

The first two blocks are the Information Technology layers where enterprise resource planning suites sit, such as customer relationship management and sales applications. Data from these tools and software is routed to the data and reporting layer for reporting purposes. The bottom two layers are the Operational Technology layers. The monitoring and control equipment (MCE) layer is where the actual production of goods or processing takes place. This is where, as an example, cars are manufactured or mining occurs, and all these are controlled and monitored by supervisory control and data acquisition (SCADA) systems. SCADA is a system of software and hardware elements that allows industrial organizations to

- Control industrial processes locally or at remote locations

- Monitor, gather, and process real-time data

- Directly interact with devices such as sensors, valves, pumps, motors, and more through human-machine interface (HMI) software

- Record events into a log file

Along with SCADA, product life cycle management tools form part of the MCE layer. Product life cycle management (PLM) refers to the management of data and processes used in the design, engineering, manufacturing, sales, and service of a product across its entire life cycle and across the supply chain.

As part of IoT, all four layers integrate with each other, thereby enabling a seamless data and information exchange between IT and OT.

The Triple Challenges in IoT

There are several reasons why IoT projects fail, one of them is lack of a business strategy toward IoT project implementation. Another reason is the lack of a well-thought approach toward security and interoperability. Though there had been a lot of efforts made since the last few years to address these three challenges for IoT, a point to be noted is that we are still far away from perfection in these areas.

Business Strategy

Several enterprises have embarked in their IoT journey by identifying IoT use cases and choosing a technology to implement those use cases. Such piecemeal IoT implementations are a definite path to failure. An IoT implementation is not a technology initiative. It is a business initiative that is achieved using technology. A business initiative is derived using a business strategy.

IoT Security

IoT means integrating IT and OT which is an emerging trend in the IT industry and is becoming more popular each and every day. Over the next few years, IoT is going to become the standard for everyone. Security and privacy are however the biggest challenges being faced today as IoT deals with a lot of devices and sensors that collect a lot of personal data about people and enterprises which is then passed to the IT systems. As an example, a smart meter knows when a person is home and what electronics individuals are using and when. All this information is shared with other devices and held in databases by companies. Some experts argue that not enough is being done to build security and privacy into the IoT ecosystem at these early stages. To prove their point further, some have even hacked a host of devices, from connected baby monitors to automated lighting and smart fridges, as well as citywide systems such as traffic signals.

A research in 2018 shows that 55% of IT professionals list security in an IoT world as their top priority. This is according to a survey conducted by 451 Research.[3] From corporate servers to cloud storage, cybercriminals are finding ways to exploit information at many points within an IT-OT ecosystem. As of 2021, many of the security challenges mentioned by these IT professionals have been addressed, but still there is a long way to go.

Definition

Critical infrastructure is the body of systems, networks, and assets that are so essential that their continued operation is required to ensure the security of a given enterprise, its economy, and employee's health and/or safety.

---

[3] https://451research.com/blog/1934-survey-finds-security-continues-to-be-top-priority-in-deploying-iot-projects

The interesting part is that hackers have not spent much time or effort so far in hacking OT devices since there are not many enterprises or people who are using IoT fully, and hence it is not worth the effort for them. This is however going to be a new area of focus for cybercriminals as enterprises start utilizing IoT in their day-to-day business. Security is one of the most important elements that needs to be addressed in an IoT implementation. The good news is that there are several mature practices that have been developed in this area. We are going to discuss about these in greater detail in subsequent chapters.

IoT Interoperability

Interoperability is a characteristic of a product or system to work with other products or systems, at present or in the future, in either implementation or access, without any restrictions.

Interoperability continues to be one of the major challenges in the IoT world. The interoperability issues in IoT can be seen from different perspectives due to heterogeneity. Heterogeneity is not a new concept nor restricted to a domain. Even in the physical world, there are many types of heterogeneities, for example, people speak dissimilar languages, but they can still communicate with each other through a translator (human/tools) or by using a common language. Likewise, the diverse elements comprising IoT (devices, communications, services, applications, etc.) should seamlessly cooperate and communicate with each other to realize the full potential of the IoT ecosystem.

Interoperability in the IoT context starts from device interoperability to network interoperability, syntactic interoperability, semantic interoperability, and platform interoperability. Though there are several solutions by IoT vendors to solve these interoperability issues, we are far from perfection, and the challenge still continues.

The industry attempts to address IoT interoperability challenges through standardization. Several efforts have emerged to establish standards for providing interoperability between IoT devices, networks, services, and data formats owned by different providers. The European Union has also recently funded several research projects under the H2020 program focusing on the federation of IoT platforms. However, it may take a long time before the related standards are fully agreed upon and accepted, if ever.

However, the good news is that if an IoT project is well planned, interoperability issues can be resolved, thereby ensuring that solutions built now can be future-proofed. To set expectations right, interoperability should be aspired specific to an industry rather than cross industries, else it will lead to disasters in IoT implementation. What this means is that the different hardware and software that are part of the IoT architecture should be interoperable to implement use cases within an industry domain such as manufacturing or retail or pharmaceutical. As an example, Gateways built for IoMT (Internet of Medical Things) should be able to communicate with sensors and devices built for hospitals and are not required to interoperate with sensors and devices used in manufacturing.

Device Interoperability

IoT is composed of a variety of devices, even more than the traditional Internet. These devices, which are called "smart objects/things," may consist of high-end devices or low-end devices. The high-end IoT devices have enough resources and computational capabilities such as smartphones. On the other hand, the low-end IoT devices are resource constrained in terms of energy, processing power, and communication capabilities than typical hosts such as RFID tags and tiny and low-cost sensors, to name a few.

The key interoperability challenge with these devices stems from the various communication protocols that these devices use. Some devices use Wi-Fi technologies and 3G/4G cellular communications to communicate, while other devices such as wearables use Bluetooth, and others such as environmental sensors use Zigbee standard.

Network Interoperability

Network interoperability is the continuous ability to send and receive data among the interconnected networks, providing the quality level expected by the end user without any negative impact to the sending and receiving networks.

The networks that IoT devices will be operating on will continue to be heterogeneous, multiservice, multivendor, and largely distributed. Different from desktop computers, IoT devices generally rely on various short-ranged wireless communication and networking technologies, which are rather more intermittent and unreliable.

Network-level interoperability deals with mechanisms to enable seamless message exchange between systems through different networks (networks of networks) for end-to-end communication. To make systems interoperable, each system should be able to exchange messages with other systems through various types of networks. Due to the dynamic and heterogeneous network environment in IoT, the network interoperability level should handle issues such as addressing, routing, resource optimization, security, QoS, and mobility support.

Semantic Interoperability

Semantic interoperability means that different agents, services, and applications are enabled to exchange information, data, and knowledge in a meaningful way, on and off the Web.[4]

---

[4] W3C, "W3C Semantic Integration & Interoperability Using RDF and OWL." [Online]. Available: www.w3.org/2001/sw/BestPractices/OEP/SemInt/. [Accessed: 25-Jul-2017]

The data generated by IoT devices are in different formats which hinders the interoperability of applications and platforms since they cannot interpret the data generated by others.

To be more precise, the data generated by things about the environment may have a defined data format (e.g., JSON, XML, or CSV), but the data formats of other devices are usually dissimilar and not always compatible. This is the biggest challenge with IoT systems.

In this context, there had been a major need for using common vocabularies capable of describing the meaning of data in this environment. In order to implement solutions that minimize the interoperability problems found in the IoT environment, several standards, languages, and approaches are being defined such as by the Semantic Web. These standards will ensure that the exchange of information is meaningful and with understandable meanings. These include semantics in data by adding self-described information packages. Semantic interoperability is used to ensure that IoT devices from different vendors are interoperable.

Though the adoption of the Internet of Things is gradually increasing, there remains a significant obstacle that hinders its adoption as a truly ubiquitous technology: the ability of devices to unambiguously exchange data with shared meaning. In this respect, the World Wide Web Consortium has developed the Web of Things architecture to provide semantic data exchange. However, such an architecture does not cover all possible use cases and still has important limitations.

Many platforms still do not address semantic interoperability, and it is one of the important areas for enterprises to validate before choosing an IoT solution.

Syntactic Interoperability

Syntactic interoperability refers to the packaging and transmission mechanisms for data.

With semantic interoperability, the data is not only exchanged between two or more systems but also understood by each system. Syntactic interoperability may be considered as a subset of semantic interoperability, which allows two or more systems to communicate and exchange data; however, the interface and programming languages may be different and need not be understood by one another.

Syntactic interoperability refers to the interoperation of the format as well as the data structure used in any exchanged information or service between heterogeneous IoT system entities. An interface needs to be defined for each resource, exposing some structure according to some schema. WSDL and REST APIs are examples. The content of the messages need to be serialized to be sent over the channel and the format to do so (such as XML or JSON). The message sender encodes data in a message using syntactic rules, specified in some grammar. The message receiver decodes the received message using syntactic rules defined in the same or some other grammar. Syntactic interoperability problems arise when the sender's encoding rules are incompatible with the receiver's decoding rules, which leads to mismatching message parse trees.

Platform Interoperability

Platform interoperability issues in IoT arise due to the availability of diverse operating systems (OSs), programming languages, data structures, architectures, and access mechanisms for things and data. There are currently many different OSs developed specifically for IoT devices, such as Contiki, RIOT, TinyOS, and OpenWSN, each with several versions. Besides, the IoT platform providers, such as Apple HomeKit, Google Brillo, Amazon AWS IoT, and IBM Watson, provide different operating systems, programming languages, and data structures. For example, Apple HomeKit supports its own open source language Swift, Google Brillo uses Weave, and Amazon AWS IoT offers SDKs for embedded C and Node.js. This non-uniformity causes hindrance for application developers to develop cross-platform and cross-domain IoT applications apart from enterprises ending up in a vendor lock-in situation.

Currently, there is no single solution to address platform interoperability. However, the BIG IoT (Bridging the Interoperability Gap of the IoT) project aims to define a standard IoT ecosystem as part of the European Platforms Initiative. As part of the project, researchers have devised an IoT ecosystem architecture to enable platform interoperability, and we can expect some platforms to be developed in the coming years that will comply with the IoT ecosystem architecture. With the current limitations in place, enterprises need to choose a platform that provides comprehensive solutions to address every use case specific to their industry.

Summary

We discussed in this chapter about IoT being one of the biggest enabler of digital transformation. IoT is all about connecting devices over the Internet, allowing them to talk to each other and many different systems, applications, and so on. The four core elements that form an IoT ecosystem are

1. Data collection – This is the process of extracting data from the devices.

2. Device integration – This means bringing together the data of all devices.

3. Real-time analytics – This means having the ability to analyze data in real time.

4. Application and process extension – This means integrating IoT data with the rest of the applications.

We also discussed the three major reasons why IoT projects
fail. The first reason is lack of a business strategy toward IoT project
implementation, and the other two reasons are lack of a well-thought
approach toward security and interoperability. Although a lot of efforts
have been made in the last few years to address these three challenges
in IoT, we are still far away from perfection. Therefore, it is essential that
enterprises deploy specific solutions wherever possible addressing these
areas to the best of their ability while embarking on their IoT journey. In
this chapter we also discussed about IIoT which is automation and data
exchange of devices in the manufacturing industry and includes cyber-
physical systems, the Internet of Things, and cloud computing. We also
discussed about IoMT, which is Internet of Medical Things. The IoMT is
a connected infrastructure of medical devices, software applications, and
health systems and services. In the next chapter, we will discuss about
the importance of defining a business strategy to be successful and how
powerful technologies such as IoT can help achieve the business strategy.

CHAPTER 2

IoT Business Strategy

There is an evolution of technologies in the market, such as mobile, analytics, the cloud, the Internet of Things, and so on, and each of these technologies is redefining the definition of digital in their own way. Interestingly, it is not a big deal to implement these technologies if it is implemented one at a time. These technologies are all nice and create some new opportunities for enterprises, but the key reason for any enterprise to embark on a digital transformation journey is because they want to be seen as a great company. And to be a great company, they need to get the basics right and then use these new technologies to make themselves more special. So along the way of this technology evolution, everyone needs to understand that it is not about individual technologies that make an enterprise great or different, but it is more about the confluence of these technologies that creates opportunities for businesses to change the way they had been doing business earlier and be more competent in the future. With the technologies we have in the market today, the technical limitations we had in the past are eliminated, and therefore enterprises can run their business much more efficiently.

The way I have seen many companies going about the technologies is that they recognize a new technology, and they think they can have a new strategy. So companies have introduced a mobile strategy, a big data strategy, a social media strategy, an Internet of Things strategy, a cloud strategy, and a cognitive computing strategy, and this is how many companies have operated so far in silos of each technology, which is a very bad idea. It is a bad idea not because these enterprises want to onboard

© Venkatesh Upadrista 2021
V. Upadrista, *IoT Standards with Blockchain*,
https://doi.org/10.1007/978-1-4842-7271-8_2

new technologies but because there is no business strategy underpinning these technologies – as an example, a mobile strategy will not make a business successful.

A business strategy is required to make an enterprise successful, and this strategy should integrate with a technology strategy that makes most sense to the enterprise and their business. As an example, a retailer whose business strategy is improved customer satisfaction may use IoT solutions to improve overall customer experience in stores.

Digital transformation is all about changes to the ways in which enterprises have been doing business traditionally. This has resulted from the use of digital technologies by either new market entrants or established competitors – and those can be competitors that were never actually your competitors before. This could mean a grocery store entering into a clothing business or the same grocery store entering into a radically different business line, such as cloud computing, for example, Amazon. Such competitors undermine the viability of your product service portfolio or your go-to-market approach. In other words, they find ways to make your customers happier than you do, by either offering them new kinds of relationships or a new product service for portfolio or a better customer experience than you do. This is called business disruption.

What this means is that for enterprises to remain relevant in the market, they need to have an integrated business strategy inspired by powerful technologies to enable them to be responsive to constant market changes, and IoT is one such powerful technology. To achieve this, every enterprise needs to adopt a start-up mindset, based on which they can start to think about a strategy that is different from what they have currently. This makes enterprises constantly respond to the changing market conditions.

This means that the traditional approach to define a strategy – where enterprises set targets on earnings per share or decide which new markets to enter or what companies to acquire – is not meaningful anymore. The business strategy in the new digital transformation world is to define how enterprises need to make themselves special in the market and how they can deliver value to their customers. This is the basic concept of the Business Transformation Model, which we will be discussing in subsequent sections.

Digital transformation revolves around the business strategy for an enterprise. Based on the business strategy, the IoT-led digital transformation road map is defined by identifying business processes that can differentiate the enterprise in the market (from their competitors) or which can improve the customer engagement for the enterprise or help enterprises to be much more efficient.

In the current market conditions, there are three business strategies for enterprises to adopt and remain relevant in their marketspace – the first is the Customer Engagement Strategy, the second is the Business Transformation Strategy, and the third is the Business Productivity Improvement Strategy. This is illustrated in Figure 2-1.

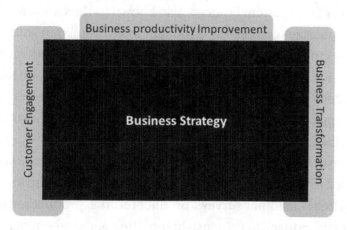

Figure 2-1. *Business Transformation Model*

From an IoT perspective, there are multiple ways to achieve success. Some companies focus on connecting existing products to make them more attractive and useful to customers, which is the Customer

Engagement Strategy. Others exploit opportunities to achieve operational improvements that increase efficiency and lower costs. Still others push more boldly, using connectivity to create entirely new products or remake business models (even moving into separate IoT businesses). My own experience has been that enterprises that achieved a scale in IoT did so by pursuing a variety of strategies – and all with at least some degree of success. However, when we looked more closely at the gains, I have seen that the most successful companies often played to their strengths – rather than betting on unfamiliar markets or new products. The enterprises getting the most economic benefit from IoT were the ones that have added IoT connectivity to existing products rather than entering into new markets or creating new IoT products or services.

Customer Engagement Strategy

The Customer Engagement Strategy, also known as the Go-to-Market Strategy, emphasizes completely on enhancing relationship with customers. It emphasizes on customer relationship to be built on trust and loyalty – ideally, built on passion. This means enterprises need to transform their Go-to-Market Strategy and keep customer relationship and customer happiness as their core fundamental driver to do business and compete in their marketspace.

In the past, the interaction between a company and its customers was restricted to the point of sale. As a result, companies were forced to collect data from customer surveys, product returns, product reviews, and anecdotal feedback to gain insight into the needs, preferences, and behaviors of their customers. This meant that companies tended to practice reactive customer engagement instead of proactive customer engagement.

Fortunately, companies are changing the way they practice customer engagement for the better, using IoT technologies, which is making it easier for companies to engage with customers and collect data in a non-intrusive way.

One of the classic examples of achieving customer engagement with IoT is proven with BMW Assist. BMW Assist (also branded as MINI Assist) is a telematic roadside assistance service offered by BMW. BMW Assist is similar to GM's OnStar or Mercedes-Benz mbrace services which uses cellular network and global positioning telemetry to locate or guide the vehicle using IoT. BMW Assist provides turn-by-turn directions, vehicle diagnostics, airbag deployment notification, theft recovery, and towing or flat tire repair. Another major feature of BMW Assist is remote unlocking – if a consumer locks their keys in their vehicle, they can call BMW Assist instead of a locksmith. In many cases, all the consumer needs to do is answer a few simple questions, and BMW will unlock the doors of the vehicle remotely. BMW Assist is an example of how IoT technologies can be used to not only boost customer engagement but also change the lives of customers for the better.

The use of IoT to enhance customer engagement was formerly limited to industrial applications. Nowadays, business-to-consumer (B2C) companies are recognizing the potential of IoT to transform customer engagement.

Businesses use IoT technologies to personalize situations for customers. IoT devices can change and refine capabilities and services based on information collected about the user's surroundings.

Through new capabilities to manage and analyze the real-time data that connected devices provide, companies are now able to gain key insights into product performance, consumer trends, and purchasing behavior, at an unprecedented speed and scale. For example, Coca-Cola's data from its Freestyle and other vending machines have enabled the company to gain valuable understanding about patterns of where, when, and how customers are purchasing and consuming their products. For example, through connected vending machines, Coca-Cola has reported that it can see spikes in its beverage consumption on college campuses before certain television shows air, a specific insight that not only leads to better understanding of customer demographics but one that also presents opportunities for targeted marketing.

Another example is with a large manufacturing company that makes engines that have sensors in them, which feed data about the engine performance. The company uses this data to improve their engine designs and detect any flaws in the existing designs. With this approach, the company is able to further optimize the performance and reliability of their products. This helps them come up with better products. If the changes are just in the configuration, they send the changes to the engine automatically over the Internet through the IoT devices. This ensures that the customers always have the best possible updated configurations of the product.

By using the IoT to make product improvements, enterprises can significantly improve customer satisfaction and tremendously impact relationships with them. Such added services help enterprises retain their customers longer.

This is what the Customer Engagement Strategy is all about. If customer engagement is not the enterprise business strategy, the next one to look at is the Business Transformation Strategy.

Business Transformation Strategy

The Business Transformation Strategy means that enterprises should move away from just thinking about the products and services they are selling. They need to think about customer needs and problems and how these can be solved by redefining their business and if required enter into new territories or business domains. The Business Transformation Strategy is broadly split into Process Transformation, Model Transformation, and Domain Transformation as depicted in Figure 2-2.

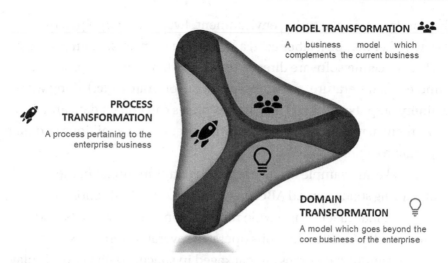

MODEL TRANSFORMATION

A business model which complements the current business

PROCESS TRANSFORMATION

A process pertaining to the enterprise business

DOMAIN TRANSFORMATION

A model which goes beyond the core business of the enterprise

Figure 2-2. *Business Transformation Strategy*

Process Transformation

Process Transformation involves an examination of the steps required to achieve a specific goal in an effort to remove duplicate or unnecessary steps and automate as many actions as possible. The end goal is to improve customer or employee satisfaction and at the same time be cheaper and efficient.

We have already seen Process Transformation on the shop floor where companies such as Airbus have engaged heads-up display glasses to improve the quality of inspection by the staff of airplanes. We have also seen Process Transformations in the customer experience, where Domino's Pizza, for example, completely reimagined the notion of food ordering, with the introduction of "AnyWare" which allowed customers to order their meals from any device. This innovation increased customer convenience so much that it helped push the company to overtake Pizza Hut in sales. We have also seen that manufacturing companies have learned that traditional manufacturing management software, such as an MES platform, that relies on humans to input data cannot keep pace with a modern manufacturing environment. Every input by a person has a cost, whether that be a labor cost, a lost production cost, or an accuracy cost. By connecting software directly to sensors that measure production parameters (temperature, pressure, speed, off/on states, etc.) along with machinery outputs and RFID chips, enterprises can collect data and analyze them in real time, thereby allowing them to save millions of dollars with predictive maintenance.

Let us take an example of a leading global multinational in the manufacturing space named ABC Productions. ABC Productions specializes in manufacturing a wide range of consumer products sold across the world. ABC Productions operates several warehouses, and products in various categories are packaged in specific delivery or display cartons at these facilities. As most CPG businesses consist of high volumes (product manufacturing, number of transactions, and storage of products) with low margins, optimizing every operation and effectively utilizing resources is the main lever for them to make profits. The key problem for ABC Productions both at the production plants and warehouses was the lack of visibility when machine breakdowns happen, or idle time occurs, thereby resulting in delays in delivery.

We were tasked to implement real-time line monitoring and an alert system to gain control over downtimes and implement improvement measures within the manufacturing units as well as warehouses. The technical specifications of this project were to implement

- A complex, wireless sensor-based tracking of line performance, along with plug-and-play sensors and hardware with minimal installation overhead

- A cloud-based, multitenant hosted platform as the single data repository for data across the warehouses and manufacturing units

- Extreme accuracy and reliability in manufacturing units, as the system would be used as a point of reference

- A highly customized application to track business KPIs along with a platform that provides the ability to easily integrate with existing IT systems

We installed wireless sensors and a hardware communication Gateway at ABC warehouses and production units. An IoT platform and a custom business application were deployed in the cloud. The IoT platform prebuilt interfaces were leveraged to integrate with all dependent systems including ERP.

The implementation resulted in several benefits to ABC Productions, some of which are listed as follows:

- Productivity improvement – The Operation Technology team was able to get real-time insight into parameters that impact line productivity, such as line rates, loss, and quality analysis at multiple levels. With these insights, predictive maintenance was performed, thereby improving line productivity by more than 35%.

- With machine health monitoring, ABC was able to monitor and analyze parameters that are critical to machine health. They were able to optimize machine downtime by predicting failure before it occurs.

- Optimized consumables – ABC was able to analyze energy and other consumables that are part of the production process and discover ways to optimize utilization.

This case study is a clear example that demonstrates that Process Transformation can create significant value, and digital transformation using IoT is becoming increasingly popular in these areas. These Process Transformations tend to focus efforts around specific areas of the business at an enterprise level and therefore are often successfully led by a combination of CIOs, CBOs, and CDOs.[1, 2]

Model Transformation

While Process Transformation focuses on finite areas of the business, Model Transformations are aimed at the fundamental building blocks of how value is delivered in the industry. Examples of this kind of innovation are well known, from Netflix's reinvention of video distribution to Apple's reinvention of music delivery (iTunes) and Uber's reinvention of the taxi industry. This kind of transformation should however be occurring in every industry, and IoT can support such a transformation. Insurance companies, such as Allstate, are using IoT with data and analytics to unbundle insurance contracts and charge customers by the mile, which is a big change to the auto insurance business model. Although not yet a reality, there are also numerous efforts underway to transform the business of mining to a wholly robotic exercise using IoT, where no humans would be required to travel below the surface.

Another most compelling model that is being discussed in the industry is the asset sharing model that is allowing enterprises to create a new business model to improve utilization of their assets and enter into a completely new business model.

An asset sharing model allows enterprises to share their costly IoT-enabled assets with other business entities or users. A clear example of an asset sharing model is the electric scooters that are now on the streets of

---

[1] The Art of Consultative Selling in IT: Taking Blue Ocean Strategy a Step Ahead Hardcover – 29 Jun. 2017 by Venkatesh Upadrista

[2] Managing Offshore Development Projects: An Agile Approach Paperback – 1 Sept. 2008 by Venkatesh Upadrista

the UK. IoT-connected devices combined with consumers' pay-per-use for a product is the model that is getting more prevalent in the world. The organization sharing the asset can charge for the asset based on the usage, time for the usage, and nature of the usage, which is similar to the outcome business model. In this model, a customer rents assets, but whatever they do not use is then fed back into the system. Instead of renting out an equipment to one customer, with asset sharing the customer has the asset for a specific amount of time. In this way, the products are circulating the market quicker, and the product is benefitting from full utilization across several customers. This also determines how long the asset is lying idle and not in use. In this use case, rather than taking the asset and only paying for the time customers use it or the outputs, customers rent the asset for a set amount of time, and when they are finished, it is then passed on to the next customer. With an IoT system, the assets are connected to the Internet to ensure they are not stolen and can be easily tracked for usage and wear and tear.

Self-driving cars and smart or virtual power plants, shared drones, and microgrids are all examples of how assets can be transferred. Toshiba has developed a virtual power plant with AI and IoT networks, mapping a power plant virtually to control the inputs and outputs and to make use of any excess supply of energy during power outages. These plants do not own the energy assets; they own the data that is transferred between each piece of equipment in the network.

The complex and strategic nature of these opportunities requires involvement and leadership by a strategy. By changing the fundamental building blocks of value, corporations that achieve model transformation open significant new opportunities for growth.

Domain Transformation

An area where we see little focus in the industry today, but which offers enormous opportunity, is the Domain Transformation.

Domain Transformation means entering into markets where enterprises were never present before, that is, new or adjacent markets.

New technologies are redefining products and services, blurring industry boundaries and creating entirely new sets of nontraditional competitors. Many enterprises do not appreciate the real opportunity for these new technologies to unlock wholly new businesses for their companies beyond currently served markets. Often, it is this type of transformation that offers the greatest opportunities to create new value. A clear example how Domain Transformation works is the online retailer Amazon. Amazon expanded into a new market domain with the launch of Amazon Web Services (AWS), now the largest cloud computing service provider, in a domain formerly owned by IT giants such as Microsoft and IBM. What made Amazon's entry into this domain possible was a combination of the strong digital capabilities it had built in storage, computing databases to support its core retail business coupled with an installed base of thousands of relationships with young, growing companies that increasingly needed computing services to expand. AWS is not a mere adjacency or business extension for Amazon, but a wholly different business in a fundamentally different marketspace.

Business Productivity Improvement

In a formal sense, productivity refers to how well an organization converts input (such as labor, materials, machines, and capital) into goods and services or output. But today it is no longer limited to measuring ratios of inputs and outputs. Increasing productivity just means working smarter, and enterprises can look for opportunities to improve efficiency just about anywhere – some may consider cost takeout by optimizing existing operations or production lines as a productivity improvement strategy, and some may want to bring improvements in their current operations by reducing manual interventions, thereby improving quality and leading to reduce cost of failures. With IoT technology comes the possibility of automation. Smart offices make use of a number of connected devices that monitor, control, and manage various operations across a business. Using these to automate repetitive tasks normally held by employees can increase efficiency and free up their time to focus on more complex work.

In addition to improving employee productivity, IoT can help businesses make more efficient use of resources and minimize unnecessary expenses. One example of this is the use of smart heating and lighting systems. Systems like the Nest Thermostat can help lower energy expenditure from overuse of air conditioning and heating.

In a supply chain world, IoT allows enterprises to track the transport and delivery of products, helping them monitor arrival times and logistics more accurately. Smart tags and sensors help keep track of inventory levels in real time and even track where an item is in a warehouse or store. This allows for more efficient stocking, which can improve companies' cash flow. More precise inventory tracking also means companies are able to reduce over-ordering and make sure the most popular products are in stock to maximize profits.

In the manufacturing sector, an IoT-empowered manufacturing process allows to monitor factory assets more easily than ever before. Smart sensors detect and notify of any issues in real time, faster than any person would. When individual components break down, companies can find them instantly based on the data they send out and replace them with ease before they cause more damage. This is particularly beneficial for running a complex operation that can be very costly to shut down when unexpected issues arise.

Choosing Between Customer Engagement, Business Transformation, and Business Productivity Improvement Strategy

Each enterprise needs to choose the appropriate business strategies discussed earlier based on which digital transformation road map using IoT needs to be defined. Though Business Productivity Improvement can be chosen as a stand-alone business strategy, I have seen many enterprises have succeeded in providing measurable results if Business Productivity Improvement is considered hand in hand with either the Customer Engagement Strategy or the Business Transformation Strategy.

It is quite essential to understand that IoT alone cannot achieve the desired business outcomes, but it does play a major role in achieving the business outcome. Let me explain this with a case study.

Customer Engagement and Business Productivity Improvement were chosen as a business strategy for one of the large American luxury department store chains named ABC Retail. This company has originated as a shoe store and evolved into a full-line retailer with departments for clothing, footwear, handbags, jewelry, accessories, cosmetics, and fragrances.

While I was living in the United States, this was my favorite store, and the reason is because this company for years has been known for outstanding customer service. ABC Retail is centered around the best customer service since the start, and no other company is able to compete with them on customer service.

Any new customer who visits ABC Retail is asked for consent to allow ABC to retrieve their (customer) social information data from the Internet with a promise to enable best customer experience to their customers. This comes with a clear commitment that no confidential data will be stored in ABC Retail local systems or shared with anyone else.

There are specific IT capabilities that were built around customer engagement for ABC Retail, where a salesman can retrieve specific data about a customer, using which he can serve his customers better. As an example, customer A walks into the store and tells a salesman that he is looking for some new trousers and shoes. The salesman comes back in a few minutes with a few dark blue trousers and a few pointed black shoes which are exactly of the same size and favorite colors of customer A. This is not a magic. The salesman was able to do that because of the capabilities that ABC Retail has created under him. ABC Retail created a totally transparent supply chain capability where each salesman within ABC Retail has access to the past events and purchases of their customers. Based on these insights, the salesman in this specific example understood that customer A has got a new job. Based on the past one-year buying patterns, he also got to know customer A's shoe and dress sizes and favorite colors, based on which he was able to track the right size and favorite color of customer A. This is the kind of customer experience we are talking about at ABC Retail that is enabled via technology.

On the other side, we implemented several IoT use cases for ABC Retail to offer more personalized shopping experiences, increase customer loyalty and satisfaction, boost sales, and also to improve inventory management. One IoT use case was targeted to improve personalization by using sensors that are fixed to product areas and are triggered by customer actions. ABC Retail would offer instant discounts, detailed product descriptions, or alternative purchases straight to the customers' mobile, in response to where they are shopping in the store or their previous buying habits.

We also deployed IoT solutions to help ABC Retail with inventory control and tracking: by fitting smart tags to packages and products, which track each item across the supply chain, including returns, to allow ABC Retail to accurately keep pace with customer demand.

ABC Retail in 2014 itself recognized the opportunities to sell through Instagram, and this company had been simply adding more and more capabilities around mobility and around social media to improve customer experience. They analyze a lot of customer data using IoT and big data and analytics to make personalized customer experience. They extend their supply chain not just to their own stores but to partners as well. This is possible because of the capabilities they have built which are the power of Customer Engagement and Business Productivity Improvement business strategies they had chosen.

Summary

In this chapter, we discussed about the three business strategies for enterprises to adopt and remain relevant in their marketspace – the first one is the Customer Engagement Strategy, the second is the Business Transformation Strategy, and the third is the Business Productivity Improvement Strategy:

- The Customer Engagement Strategy, also known as the Go-to-Market Strategy, emphasizes completely on enhancing relationship with customers.

- The Business Transformation Strategy means that enterprises should move away from just thinking about the products and services they are selling. They need to think about customer needs and problems and how these can be solved by redefining their business and if required enter into new territories or business domains.

- The Business Productivity Improvement Strategy means looking for opportunities to improve efficiency just about anywhere in the enterprise, such as cost takeout by optimizing existing operations or production lines or by bringing improvements in their current operations by reducing manual interventions.

Once a business strategy is chosen, enterprises then apply IoT to achieve the business goals. The IoT road map is defined by identifying specific business processes which can either differentiate the enterprise in the market (from their competitors) or improve the customer engagement for the enterprise or help enterprises to be more efficient.

In the next chapter, we will discuss about the Business Transformation Model, using which business processes that have an impact on the business strategy are chosen for transformation using IoT.

CHAPTER 3

IoT Standards Business Transformation Model

Cost optimization had been a driving factor in the IT industry for decades, and most enterprises are looking at ways to reduce their costs to the best of their abilities, without compromising the quality of services they provide. Today, with digital in the forefront, enterprises are not only achieving cost targets on optimizations but are also able to achieve speed of delivery and exceed customer experiences.

Cost optimization is one of the drivers enterprises consider for digital transformation, and indeed IoT is playing a major role. However, it is important to understand that the digital transformation journey should not be embarked just for optimizing costs in an enterprise. Digital transformation journeys are embarked by a need for enterprises to do business differently and adapt to any changing business needs in the most agile way. Business transformation means changing the way enterprises interact with their customers or businesses and at the same time improving operations to become fast and cheap.

As digital technologies dramatically reshape industries, many enterprises are pursuing large-scale change efforts to capture the benefits of these trends or simply to survive in the market. It is critical

© Venkatesh Upadrista 2021
V. Upadrista, *IoT Standards with Blockchain*,
https://doi.org/10.1007/978-1-4842-7271-8_3

to embrace the dynamic landscape, as new economic opportunities are continually opening for organizations that need to quickly build and scale robust environments. Transforming the entire operations of an enterprise is extremely complex and can present a significant risk if not executed correctly. Without the right guidance and experience, it is all too easy to focus purely on technology adoption to drive the successful implementation of digital transformation strategy, overlooking the impact the changes will have on the rest of the organization. The result is high implementation costs, missed project deadlines, and an inability to see a return on investment. The concepts laid out in this book provide enterprises with the knowledge and direction necessary to achieve the business strategy by leading technology transformation using IoT. It has step-by-step and practical solutions to overcome complex problems encompassing people, processes, and technology based on the business transformation required in an enterprise.

IoT Standards is a model that enables enterprises to use IoT as a lever to create new or modify existing business processes, culture, and customer experiences to meet changing business and market requirements. This reimagining of business in the digital age is digital transformation.

There are numerous IT services companies that claim to transform organizations to digital using IoT for work they are contracted. Piecemeal digital transformations are quite dangerous, as they typically end up adding new complexities, thereby making the IT landscape much more cumbersome. On the other hand, many enterprises treat digital transformation as a pure technology stuff, whereas the real definition of digital transformation is thinking how an organization should use modern technologies, people, and processes to fundamentally change business performance.

A digital transformation journey is a top-down rather than a bottom-up approach and is successful only if it is done at an enterprise level. This does not mean that organizations need to embark on a digital transformation journey and make big changes to their already existing

IT and OT systems, tools, and processes. What this means is that digital transformation should be embarked by utilizing a well-defined enterprise-level digital transformation methodology. Without an enterprise-level methodology, enterprises cannot succeed in their efforts toward digital transformation, and IoT Standards addresses just this. IoT Standards is an enterprise-wide digital transformation model that empowers all types of organizations to embark on digital transformation journeys using IoT, thereby allowing enterprises to achieve the full benefits of digital at scale by first understanding the business drivers behind the transformation and then enabling transformation using IoT. The results of IoT Standards implementation are achieving greater alignment and visibility across the organization, connecting the business strategy to execution, and enabling better business results faster and with a higher degree of predictability and quality, with a lower operational cost.

The end results of implementing IoT Standards within an enterprise provide several of the benefits listed as follows:

- Improved customer experience and business satisfaction

- Improved efficiency of machines and shop floor staff

- Enhanced forecasting and predictive maintenance

- Enhanced product quality

- Reduced downtime

- Faster and informed decisions

- Faster time to market

- Ability to make business decisions from data

- Reduced OPEX and CAPEX costs (with automation)

- Increased ease and speed of doing business

What's Next After Business Strategy Is Chosen

After a business strategy is chosen, the next step is to identify existing core business processes of the enterprise which impact the business strategy. Potential problems and opportunities within these business processes determine the transformation journey required for these business processes. It is not always necessary that IoT is a solution to address every business problem or opportunity. There will be many instances where IoT needs to be complemented with other technology solutions to address the business problem or opportunity.

Figure 3-1 depicts the two quadrants of the Business Transformation (BT) Model. Each of the business processes is classified into the IT Zone or the IoT Zone, after which problems and opportunities within the business processes are identified.

A problem is a gap or an inefficiency within the business process which needs to be resolved or overcome. Problems can be impacting the business process currently or may impact in future and may prevent the business process from working efficiently to achieve the desired business process goals. In some cases, problems also threaten the long-term survival of the business.

An opportunity in a business process is improvements that can enhance the business process to perform much more efficiently. An opportunity that can help to meet the business process goals for increasing profits, reducing costs, or enhancing customer experience and accelerating innovation.[1]

---

[1] Formula 4.0 for Digital Transformation, A Business-Driven Digital Transformation Framework for Industry 4.0 – May 27, 2021, by Venkatesh Upadrista

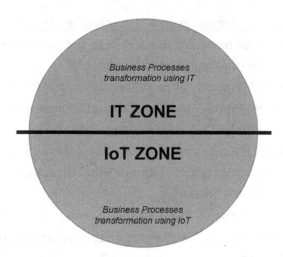

Figure 3-1. *Business Transformation Model dual quadrants*

The core business process that does not need IoT to address the problems and opportunities identified within the business processes is placed in the IT Zone.

As an example, Mart A is a retailer corporation that operates a chain of hypermarkets, discount department stores, and grocery stores. The two core IT business processes for Mart A are listed as follows:

- Business process 1 – Placing orders from ecommerce systems via a web application

- Business process 2 – Processing order information

An opportunity is identified within business process 1. The opportunity is to develop a new channel (e.g., mobile) to enhance customer engagement. Currently, there is only one channel (Web) for customer to place an order.

A problem is identified within business process 2. The problem states that there are too many manual interventions required to complete an order. This is because multiple applications were built using different technologies which do not integrate with each other. In simple terms, the output of one application needs to be manually fed into other applications to complete the order processing business process.

The problem and opportunity identified for business process 1 and business process 2 can be addressed without the need for IoT and therefore are placed in the IT Zone. In other words, the problems and opportunities within these business processes can be addressed with Information Technology or pure IT solutions and therefore are not considered part of the IoT road map.

The core business process that aligns to the chosen business strategy and which will use IoT to address the problems and opportunities is placed in the IoT Zone.

Let me explain this with a case study. A large fleet management company tasked us to define a digital transformation road map for their organization. The company chose Business Transformation and Business Productivity Improvement as their core business strategy. One of the core business processes identified for transformation is called "on-time delivery of quality products at optimal costs." The company business is to deliver fresh groceries for US retail stores, such as Walmart and Aldi. This business process depicts that goods are shipped from product manufacturer locations to retail stores using trucks fitted with diesel-fired fridge units to keep the products fresh. The level 1 business process is further broken down into use cases as follows:

- Track transit time and routes to deliver goods from source to destination (UC1)

- Monitor refrigerators to keep the products fresh (UC2)

- Track and manage fuel consumption from source to destination (UC3)

- Manage operations of the trucks (UC4) and so on...

Problems (P) and opportunities (O) are identified within each use case, a few of which are stated as follows:

- A problem within use case 2 or P-UC2 – Drivers need to periodically check and control the temperature of the refrigerators. There had been instances where products have lost quality due to mismanagement of the refrigerators.

- P-UC3 and P-UC4 – Low tire pressure and faulty engines have led to excess fuel consumption between 5% and 20%, including increasing maintenance costs of trucks.

- P-UC4 – There is no proper mechanism to track and trace trucks.

IoT solutions are identified to address the problems and opportunities for the use cases. The following IoT solutions (high-level view) were defined for problems and opportunities identified for each of the use cases:

- Monitor refrigerators (e.g., temperature with each compartment) by installing temperature sensors that can be monitored and controlled from a central location without any manual action required by the driver. This will address the product freshness problem.

- Monitor engines and tires to improve fuel efficiency and truck ROI by installing sensors both at the engine level and the tire level.

- Install a track-and-trace IoT solution to optimize logistic operations.

This is a simple case study on how a business strategy is achieved with IoT use cases based on the problems and opportunities identified within the business processes.

The IoT Use Case Reference Model (IoT UCR Model)

As a best practice, it is essential to implement IoT solutions for a use case based on the impact it delivers to the enterprise. A model called the IoT Use Case Reference (UCR) Model is defined as depicted in Figure 3-2 to enable enterprises to make the right prioritization of implementing an IoT solution.

After use cases are identified for each of the business processes, each of these use cases is assessed from a complexity and impact perspective and plotted in one of the four quadrants of the IoT UCR Model.[2]

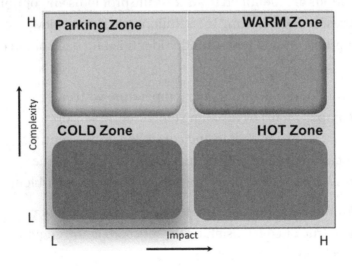

Figure 3-2. *IoT Use Case Reference Model*

---

[2] Formula 4.0 for Digital Transformation, A Business-Driven Digital Transformation Framework for Industry 4.0 – May 27, 2021, by Venkatesh Upadrista

Use cases which have high impact on the business strategy with low implementation cost and complexity are placed in the Hot zone. These are use cases that can be implemented for faster business results and are ideal candidates for pilots. My advice for young enterprises (less than 15 years in business) is to first implement use cases in the Hot zone to gain faster business and board confidence on the success that IoT can generate to their business. Use cases which have high impact on the business strategy but come with high implementation cost and complexity are placed in the Warm zone. For large or legacy enterprises, a combination of use cases in Hot and Warm zones is recommended for implementation to gain business and board confidence on the success of IoT to their business. This is because for large enterprises, there will be very limited use cases that can fit into the Hot zone.

Many companies become frustrated when they do not see early signs of transformative impact from an IoT pilot. We all need to understand that a single use case just would not prove the benefits of IoT. It has to be implemented at scale both in terms of the number of use cases and the breadth to demonstrate the impact. More widespread implementation of IoT use cases forces a cultural shift and provides new perspectives to the board and business on the benefits of IoT. In a ripple effect, this momentum often also exposes weakness in technology along with gaps in talent, both in terms of in-house IoT skill levels and the numbers of experts needed to implement IoT at scale. The "go big" approach may seem counterintuitive, particularly among enterprises that have fewer resources to deploy and feel more comfortable focusing on a small number of use cases. While a smaller scale may be good for very early days, there is a clear learning curve that companies achieve as they add use cases, and the sooner the learnings are achieved, the better it is for the enterprise. I have personally experienced that a greater number of use cases correlate with economic success regardless of the use case or type of company.

As soon as leaders are able to appreciate the benefits that IoT can bring to their enterprise, the next set of use cases that form part of the Warm zone will prove the worth of IoT if implemented at scale. As discussed, use cases that are complex but at the same time have high impact to achieve the business objective are placed in the Warm zone. Complexity may be complemented with an increasing cost, but at the same time these are use cases that have much higher impact on the business strategy.

At one of the large manufacturing companies, it was a cherishing moment that the board level executives supported me when I realized and told them that the IoT deployment strategy which we originally designed is not bold enough. We initially decided to deploy IoT with six use cases (called minimum viable products or MVPs in this organization) from the Hot zone, but soon I realized that this narrow focus will not improve performance as much as expected, neither will we be able to achieve the outcomes that the board will appreciate. A few leaders from across the enterprise pushed against voices of caution and expanded the number of MVPs to 15, and we went to an extent to select a few MVPs from the Warm zone. Executives also found that giving managers a larger number of IoT use cases to oversee focused their attention on creating a bias to make IoT a success. That momentum built on itself as the company's best talent wanted to be part of the innovative push using IoT. A strong base of 21 IoT scrum teams was formed for these 15 MVPs which helped loosen bureaucratic decision-making rules. Finally, unexpected efficiencies turned up as engineers were able to reuse similar data architectures for multiple MVPs and found numerous synergies with each other. At the end, such an aggressive IoT use case strategy produced new revenue streams as well as improved the business process efficiencies between 60% and 80% and reduced costs between 28% and 67% for the specific business processes that these 15 MVPs were part of.

The Cold zone is a zone where low impact and low complex use cases are placed. Enterprises typically choose uses cases from this zone for implementation once they have implemented all use cases within the Hot zone and the Warm zone. Some use cases that have dependencies on use cases from the Hot and Warm zones are also placed in this zone which are called the use case subsets. With a combination of the use cases in the Hot and Warm zones, the use case subsets (i.e., dependent use case) in the Cold zone can generate additional value to enterprises.

Use cases which deliver minimum value but carry high complexity are placed in the Parking zone, and these are the ones which are not candidates for IoT implementations.

Applying IoT Treatments on Use Cases

Using the IoT UCR Model, we have identified use cases that form part of the IoT journey by categorizing them into the IoT Zone. IoT Standards recommends two types of treatments to the use cases that are placed in the IoT Zone. The first treatment is called the "Heterogeneous IoT Transform," and the second is the "Homogeneous IoT Transform."

Heterogeneous IoT Transform

The Heterogeneous IoT Transform is applied on use cases where an IoT solution will alone not be sufficient to achieve the business results. In other words, there would be a need for IT Application transformation of an existing legacy application along with implementing the IoT solution to achieve the business outcome from the use case.

An IT Application transformation means that applications surrounding the IoT use cases need to be digitally transformed to achieve the results. Examples of IT Application transformation could be that an application on the legacy platform needs to be refactored (rewritten) using modern technology stacks to address the problems or opportunities identified within the business process based on which the use cases have been defined.

Definition

*A **legacy system** is an old method, technology, computer system, or application program. The implication is that the system is out of date or in need of replacement. Typical characteristics of a legacy system are the following:*

1. Skills are hard to find in the market.

2. Technology is not in use for new developments.

3. The system is hard to extend with new features and takes a long time to develop a new feature.

4. Limited built-in automation capabilities.

***Refactoring**, also called **rewriting** or **modernizing**, means that the complete applications need to be redesigned and rebuilt. Often, it means that you may have to rewrite the application logic completely and develop the cloud-native version from scratch.*

A large retail customer in Europe named XYZ Retail came to us with smart store use cases, out of which one was for their scan-and-go application.[3] A scan-and-go is a modern shopping technique where a customer can scan items as they shop using their mobile phones or a specific device provided by the store and then do self-checkout without the need of a store cashier.

Customers may be drawn to the autonomy and time savings scan-and-go checkout promises, but distractions such as rambunctious kids increase the chance that customers forget to scan products and walk out of the store

---

[3] Managing Your Outsourced IT Services Provider: How to Unleash the Full Potential of Your Global Workforce Paperback – 15 Dec. 2014 by Venkatesh Upadrista

with free merchandise, potentially costing grocers a lot of losses. Retailers employ various safeguards, including front-end audits, but these all too often fail to flag unscanned items.

In an analysis published last year of more than 140 million scan-and-go transactions across 13 major retailers in the United States and the UK,[4] it was found that there were product losses of as much as 10 basis points for every 1% of sales in the scan-and-go side. That means if a store did 10% of their sales through scan-and-go, product losses could go up an additional 1%. According to the National Retail Federation,[5] retailers currently lose around 1.4% of their product stock each year through theft, employee error, and other factors, equaling more than $50 billion. Considering the already thin margins grocers operate, an additional loss of up to 1% could be a significant blow.

The use case we implemented for XYZ Retail is to detect thefts with customers using scan-and-go by introducing an IoT-led intervention solution at the self-serve checkout. As part of the solution, we adopted video analytics for cashier checkouts to be applied to self-checkouts as well. The video analytics solution proactively monitors the self-checkouts to detect the various forms of theft specific to self-checkouts and alert store personnel over their mobile in case it recognizes an irregular pattern.

The common types of irregular patterns that were addressed as part of the self-checkout kiosk use case include

- Direct to bag – The customer moves the item directly into the shopping bag, but avoids the bag weight scale.

- Price look-up (PLU) abuse – Miskeyed PLU codes.

- Unscanned items left in the cart/basket.

---

[4] www.grocerydive.com/news/theft-is-a-major-risk-for-retailers-using-scan-and-go-expert-says/563702/

[5] https://nrf.com/media-center/press-releases/retail-shrink-tops-50-billion-cyber-threats-become-more-priority

- Bypassing the belt.

- Involving the attendant.

Though the video analytics solution using IoT was a very impressive solution, the legacy mobile application named "Alerting App" which stores the personnel use to receive alerts was not capable of receiving real-time alerts. This defeats the whole idea of implementing this use case, and therefore an IT Application modernization was performed on the Alerting App in parallel to implementing an IoT solution. The Alerting App was rewritten using modern technology stack, thereby enabling real-time alerts to store personnel.

This is called the Heterogeneous IoT Transform. In the Heterogeneous IoT Transform, apart from using IoT solutions to implement the use case, IT applications are also digitally transformed (rewritten) to achieve the desired benefits from the use case.

Homogeneous IoT Transform

The Homogeneous IoT Transform is applied on use cases where an IoT solution is self-sufficient to achieve the business results from the use case. In the preceding scan-and-go case study for XYZ Retail, if an IT Application modernization of the Alerting App would not have been required, it would be called a Homogeneous IoT Transform.

Summary

After a business strategy is chosen, the next step is to identify existing core business processes of the enterprise which impact the business strategy. Potential problems and opportunities within these business processes determine the transformation road map for the enterprise.

In this chapter, we discussed about the Business Transformation (BT) Model where every business process is classified into one of the two zones, that is, the IT Zone or the IoT Zone, after which problems and opportunities within the business processes are identified, and IoT is then applied on business processes that are part of the IoT Zone.

We also discussed about the IoT Use Case Reference (UCR) Model which is a model to enable enterprises to make the right prioritization of implementing an IoT solution. Subsequently, we discussed about the two IoT treatment models, namely, the Heterogeneous IoT Transform and the Homogeneous IoT Transform. The Heterogeneous IoT Transform is applied on use cases where an IoT solution will alone not be sufficient to achieve the business results. The Homogeneous IoT Transform is applied on use cases where an IoT solution is self-sufficient to achieve the business results from the use case.

In the next chapter, we will discuss about the IoT Standard Reference Model which is a technical framework for implementing IoT use cases.

PART II

The IoT Standards Reference Model

In this part, we will discuss about the IoT Standards Reference Model which is an abstract framework consisting of an interlinked set of clearly defined components, using which enterprises can successfully implement an IoT solution.

We will also discuss the challenges faced by enterprises while implementing IoT use cases and how to overcome those using the IoT Standards Reference Model. Subsequently, we will discuss the specific principles based on which enterprises can choose appropriate devices, Smart IoT Gateway, and IoT Cloud Platform for their IoT use cases and mitigate these challenges.

CHAPTER 4

The IoT Standards Reference Model

The number of devices connected to the Internet, including the machines, sensors, and cameras that make up the Internet of Things (IoT), continues to grow at a steady pace.[1] A new forecast from IDC estimates that there will be 41.6 billion connected IoT devices, or "things," generating 79.4 zettabytes (ZB) of data in 2025.

As the number of connected IoT devices grows, the amount of data generated by these devices also grow. Some of this data is small and bursty, indicating a single metric of a machine's health, while large amounts of data are generated by several other devices such as video surveillance cameras using computer vision to analyze crowds of people, for example.

There is an obvious direct relationship between all the "things" and the data these things create. IDC projects that the amount of data created by these connected IoT devices will see a compound annual growth rate (CAGR) of 28.7% over the 2018–2025 forecast period. Most of the data is being generated by video surveillance applications, but other categories such as industrial and medical will increasingly generate more data over time.

As the market continues to mature, IoT increasingly becomes the fabric enabling the exchange of information from "things," people, and

---

[1] www.idc.com/getdoc.jsp?containerId=US45066919

© Venkatesh Upadrista 2021
V. Upadrista, *IoT Standards with Blockchain*,
https://doi.org/10.1007/978-1-4842-7271-8_4

processes. Data becomes the common denominator – as it is captured, processed, and used from the nearest and farthest edges of the network to create value for industries, governments, and individuals' lives.

The domain of the Internet of Things encompasses a wide range of technologies, and therefore a single architecture cannot be used for all possible IoT implementations. An IoT implementation differs from enterprise to enterprise. As an example, IoT for manufacturing (IIoT) is different from an IoT implementation in the healthcare sector (IoMT). In fact, IoT is like an umbrella around all possible Internet and non-Internet-enabled devices and computers around us. Therefore, the IoT architecture needs to be open enough with open protocols to support a variety of existing network applications and use cases. Additionally, middleware for scalability, security, and semantic representation should also be included to promote devices and data integration from various devices.

In this chapter, the IoT Standards Reference Model is defined which is an abstract framework or domain-specific ontology consisting of an interlinked set of clearly defined components, using which enterprises can successfully implement an IoT solution. The IoT Standards Reference Model can be applied for IoT use cases across any industries. The IoT Standards Reference Model is kept abstract in order to enable many, potentially different, IoT architectures to be implemented based on the IoT Standards reference model.

The IoT Standards Reference Model

To embark on an IoT journey, enterprises need to choose the right devices that will be part of the IoT implementation along with choosing the right networks to use, the right IoT platforms, and so on. And then finally integration needs to be done in the most secured way. The good news is that by paying attention to security early, enterprises can design security up front, rather than act reactively.

Figure 4-1 depicts the IoT Standards Reference Model, which is broadly split into three horizontal services.[2] Security is a vertical service which is applied across all the horizontal services and is one of the most important aspects to be considered while making decisions about devices, Smart IoT Gateways, or Full Stack IoT Platforms. Device Management and Artificial Intelligence (AI) are two specific services that are either part of the Smart IoT Gateway or Full Stack IoT Platform. The choice of where these services should reside is dependent on the IoT use cases and is therefore considered as a vertical within the reference model. Finally, Blockchain is an overarching function that powers the complete IoT Standards Reference Model and is a horizontal service that spans across all horizontal and vertical services.

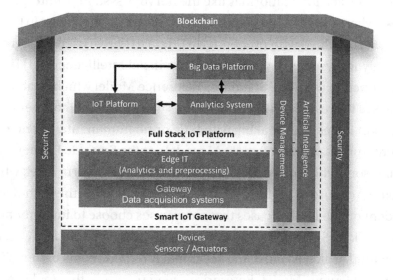

Figure 4-1. *IoT Standards Reference Model*

---

[2] www.opengroup.org/iot/wp-refarchs/p2.htm

The first horizontal service is the device layer, which consists of the physical objects that are located on the shop floors.

The second is the Smart IoT Gateway, which is responsible for collecting data from devices and relaying it to the rest of the systems. In many scenarios, the Smart IoT Gateway performs the preprocessing of the data collected from devices including analytics. Another feature the Smart IoT Gateway performs is Device Management. Some enterprises choose to perform Device Management at the Smart IoT Gateway level, but others prefer to perform Device Management in the next block which is at the Full Stack IoT Platform level. Device Management, which is discussed in detail in subsequent sections, refers to the processes involving the provisioning and authenticating, configuring, maintaining, monitoring, and diagnosing of devices operating as part of an IoT environment.

The Full Stack IoT Platform is like the nervous system of enterprise business where the IoT data coming from devices via the Smart IoT Gateway is combined with other non-IoT data to derive useful insights using analytics systems or applications.[3] Artificial Intelligence (AI) is another function in an IoT Standards Reference Model which enables **enterprises to** create **intelligent** machines that simulate smart behavior and support in decision-making with little or no human interference. Some enterprises choose to apply AI models at the Smart IoT Gateway level, and some choose to do it at the Full Stack IoT Platform level, while a few others choose to perform AI at both places. Making these choices is dependent on the IoT use cases that enterprises choose to implement.

The devices, Smart IoT Gateways, and Full Stack IoT Platform need to be secured, which is one of the key implicit requirements of the IoT Standards Reference Model. Enterprises need to ensure that tools and platforms which are chosen as part of the IoT Standards Reference Model are validated on security thoroughly.

---

[3] www.iot.org.au/wp/wp-content/uploads/2016/12/IoT-Reference-Framework-v1.0.pdf

Finally, the IoT Standards Reference Model is powered by Blockchain as a technology. Though Blockchain is currently evolving in the context of IoT, it is quite essential that enterprises plan the function while deciding their IoT architecture as Blockchain is going to become the most important element for enterprises to succeed with IoT in the future.

We are going to discuss in detail each of these functions in subsequent chapters, and a quick preview is provided as follows.

Devices (the Sensors and Actuators)

As the basis for every IoT system, connected devices or connected objects are responsible for providing data, which is the essence of the Internet of Things. To pick up physical parameters in the outside world or within the object itself, devices need sensors.

Fundamentally, an IoT device is composed of hardware and software with an operating system, a compute, storage, and connectivity. The big difference between a device and a computer is that the inputs and outputs for an IoT device are very different from a traditional computer. Devices constitute of sensors and actuators.

Sensors are either embedded in the devices themselves or implemented as stand-alone objects to measure and collect telemetry data. For an example, the task of agricultural sensors is to measure parameters such as air and soil temperature and humidity, soil pH levels, or crop exposure to sunlight.

Not all IoT devices are going to have outputs. The ones that have outputs can perform actions for an event, such as letting somebody know something has happening for a buzzer press or an output can be a hydraulic lift lifting several tons once a button is pressed.

Another element of this layer is the actuators. Working in close collaboration with the sensors, actuators transform the data generated by devices into physical action. As an example, imagine a smart watering system with all the necessary sensors in place. Based on the input provided by the sensors, the device analyzes the situation in real time and commands the actuators to open selected water valves located in places where soil humidity is below the set value. The valves are kept open until the sensors report that the values are restored to default.

It is essential for devices to remain connected so that they can transmit and receive data and execute instructions.

In the new connected devices' world, it is also essential that devices talk to other devices to gather and share information and collaborate in real time to leverage the value of the whole IoT deployment. It is not always possible to achieve this objective, and workarounds need to be created, since there are many legacy devices in enterprises which are resource constrained and battery operated – the communication of one device to others requires lots of resources such as computing power, energy, and bandwidth, which these legacy devices are challenged with. In addition to these constraints, each device communicates in a different language (called a protocol), and therefore it is not always easy for devices to directly talk to each other. This is the main reason why Smart IoT Gateways have come into play and are the workaround for any device, be it modern or legacy, to communicate with other devices in the most secure and optimal fashion.

Smart IoT Gateways

Smart IoT Gateways typically perform three major functions as depicted in Figure 4-2.[4]

---

[4] Formula 4.0 for Digital Transformation, A Business-Driven Digital Transformation Framework for Industry 4.0 – May 27, 2021, by Venkatesh Upadrista

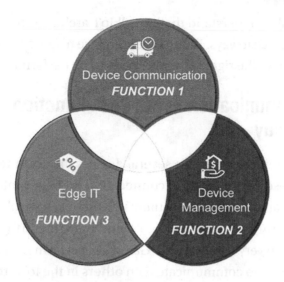

Figure 4-2. *Functions of a Smart IoT Gateway*

Firstly, it acts as the data acquisition layer and enables devices to communicate and share data with each other and with the rest of the systems in an IoT architecture, and secondly it performs the management of IoT devices. The reason why IoT Gateways are called Smart is because they perform another important function which is the preprocessing of the data received from IoT devices and analytics which is also referred as Edge IT or Analytics at the edge.

Not all IoT Gateways are smart. A standard IoT Gateway is one which just performs the first function which is to enable device communication. Some Gateway manufacturers enable their Gateways to perform Device Management. A Smart Gateway performs data processing and analytics at the Gateway level, reducing overhead of sending and receiving data to the IoT Platform. It brings computation and data storage closer to the location where devices reside, to improve response times and save network bandwidth.

It is essential to understand that not all IoT architecture will need to have Smart IoT Gateways. Based on enterprise needs and the IoT use cases, a selection of the right Gateway needs to be performed.

Device Communication Is the First Function of the Gateway

In an IoT ecosystem, there will be several devices that an enterprise will have, and all these devices need to connect and exchange information. Not all devices can directly talk to others because each speaks a different language (aka communication protocol), and therefore IoT (Smart) Gateways become very essential. IoT Gateways perform the function of enabling devices to communicate with others in the IoT architecture irrespective of the communication protocols they use. We will discuss more about communication protocols in Chapter 6.

The IoT (Smart) Gateway indicates that the Gateway could be an IoT Gateway or an Smart IoT Gateway.

The IoT Gateway means that the Gateway does not have the smart features, that is, it does not have the data storage, data preprocessing, and analytics capabilities.

A communication protocol is a system of rules that allow two or more entities of a communications system to transmit information.

An IoT (Smart) Gateway is a solution for enabling IoT communications, usually device-to-device communications or device-to-cloud communications. IoT Gateways are devices that perform functions such as protocol translation to a common standard, data processing, data storage, data filtering, and device security.

Given the massive volume of input and output that millions of devices generate, capabilities for the aggregation, selection, and transportation of data are very essential. As intermediaries between the connected things and the cloud and analytics, Gateways act as data acquisition systems and provide the necessary connection points that tie the remaining layers together. IoT Gateways facilitate communications between the sensors and the rest of the systems by converting the sensor data into formats that are easily transferable and usable for other system components.

Device Management Is Another Essential Function Performed by Some Gateways

Device Management is the process of automatically and securely provisioning, authenticating, configuring, controlling, monitoring, and maintaining the IoT devices. Some enterprises choose to perform Device Management by an IoT (Smart) Gateway, and some prefer to use the Full Stack IoT Platform to perform Device Management based on the specific use cases which enterprises target to implement.

Edge Computing Is the Third Important Function for Smart IoT Gateways

Edge computing is a distributed computing paradigm that brings together computation and data storage closer to the location where it is needed, to improve response times and save bandwidth.

Edge computing is transforming the way data is being handled, processed, and delivered from millions of devices around the world. The explosive growth of Internet-connected devices – the IoT – along with new applications that require real-time computing power, continues to drive edge computing systems.

Faster networking technologies, such as 5G wireless, are allowing for edge computing to accelerate the creation or support of real-time applications, such as video processing and analytics, self-driving cars, Artificial Intelligence, and robotics, to name a few.

Definitions

Workloads *is a term used within this book which is a combination of applications, connectivity, and data either in full or in parts.*

In a network, latency measures the time it takes for some data to get to its destination across the network. It is usually measured as a round-trip latency, which is the time taken for information to get to its destination and back again to the source.

Gartner defines edge computing as "a part of a distributed computing topology in which information processing is located close to the edge, where things and people produce or consume that information." At a basic level, edge computing brings computation and data storage closer to the devices where it is being gathered, rather than relying on a central location that can be thousands of miles away. This means that data, especially real-time data, is processed by the Smart IoT Gateways which are hosted near to the location where devices reside. Because of this, enterprises do not face latency issues since data is shared back and forth and processed near to the devices. In addition, with Smart IoT Gateways, companies can save money because processing is carried out locally which reduces the amount of data that needs to be sent and processed in a centralized or cloud-based location.

Smart IoT Gateways which are enabled with edge computing have gained a lot of importance due to the exponential growth of IoT devices, which connect to the Internet for either receiving information from the cloud or delivering data back to the cloud. Many IoT devices generate enormous amounts of data during the course of their operations.

Smart IoT Gateways are primarily about moving processing away from the cloud, closer to the end device or end user. This also incorporates latency for time-sensitive applications, such as those within IoT which need real-time responses.

The key drivers of edge computing with Smart IoT Gateways are

- Network and bandwidth – Edge computing can minimize the cost of moving large amounts of data, plus reducing reliance on the network.

- Data privacy and security – Edge computing helps organizations comply with data sovereignty laws and makes sure intellectual property remains on-premises.

- Adoption of edge computing is also being driven by a desire to make local computing – on devices or on-premises.

- On round-trip latency issues, edge computing has disrupted the complete market. The cloud is all about accessing systems on the Internet, which means data and communication need to be moved back and forth over the Internet. With edge computing, data resides with the Smart IoT Gateway which mitigates the network latency issues.

Though one may not see an edge device as part of every IoT architecture, this is one of the most important element that will determine the future success of any IoT implementation done today for specific enterprises and use cases. Edge computing brings significant benefits especially to large-scale IoT implementations.

Challenges with Smart Gateways

Smart IoT Gateways are enabled with edge computing that provides data storage and compute power. They perform processing of data at the Gateway itself, but there is a limit to the amount of data and compute that can be done at the Gateway level. Enterprises that have millions of devices connected to the Gateways and that need massive compute capabilities need to make choices on what data need to be processed at the Smart IoT Gateway level, and the rest of the data and processing needs to be performed by the Full Stack IoT Platform which typically resides in the cloud.

To overcome the limitation on data storage and compute at the IoT Edge Gateway level, there are enterprises that are experimenting specialized models to provide limitless compute capability near to the Smart IoT Gateways or devices. These companies are trying to maintain and manage servers regionally that will ensure that enterprises do not need to move the workload back and forth on the Internet, thereby committing the latency which the application and the business teams within an enterprise are looking from the cloud. In addition, these companies are going further and allowing to connect applications and data spread across multiple cloud providers (e.g., AWS, Azure, or Google Cloud) and across private and public clouds. This is especially important for larger enterprises that choose to set up their own private cloud in a colocation environment for mission-critical or sensitive applications and data, and move the rest to a public cloud. The need to collaborate and communicate between the private cloud and the public cloud is enabled by these companies. One such example is Cloud Interconnect Fabric by Equinix.

A number of private and public cloud providers are highly engaged in making limitless edge computing a success.

Siemens have come up with the concept of industrial edge. Industrial edge solution allows enterprises to analyze all the data at the machine and at the same time to preprocess the data quickly and instantly. The optimized data points can then be transferred to the cloud where enterprises have access to more computing power and larger storage capacities.

Full Stack IoT Platform

The Full Stack IoT Platform is designed to store, process, and analyze large volumes of data for deeper insights using powerful data analytics engines and machine learning mechanisms. It is a platform to create and manage applications, run analytics, and store and secure enterprise IoT data. Some enterprises choose to perform Device Management at the IoT Platform level, which depends on the use case being considered, and in all such cases, the right IoT Platform needs to be chosen that can support this feature.

There are multiple IoT platforms that are existing in the market today, and most of these platforms support Device Management. There are platforms for specific industries like commercial real estate and family health. Some focus on one type of device: for example, there are at least a couple of platforms focused on augmented reality headsets. Some are focused on a particular function, like manufacturing, and some for healthcare.

There is no one-size-fits-all Full Stack IoT Platform that can be used across any industry or can solve any business problem; therefore, to choose the right IoT platform, one needs to start with a good understanding of the enterprise IoT strategy, the kinds of problems and opportunities enterprises are trying to address via IoT (and respective use cases), and the primary industry of the enterprise such as manufacturing, retail, or healthcare. Based on this, an IoT platform needs to be chosen.

Any IoT platform should be able to follow data through the journey starting from gathering data from devices (using the Smart IoT Gateways) to generating insights from the data. The key to transform data from a device into an IoT platform begins with very specific data that comes from a machine-specific industrial protocol or healthcare device, and as it ingested into the platform, data is processed, normalized, and standardized to a structure that is well suited for the analytics platform to generate insights. This is one of the reasons an IoT Platform with a very strong data and analytics capability needs to be chosen that can support generating the right insights from the vast data that is pumped from the devices.

AI (Artificial Intelligence) Is an Important Function Performed by the IoT Platform and in Some Cases Performed at the IoT Gateway Level (Called Edge IT)

Artificial Intelligence forms one of the most important features in an IoT Standards Reference Model.

Artificial Intelligence (AI) refers to the simulation of human intelligence in machines that are programmed to think like humans and mimic their actions. The term may also be applied to any machine that exhibits traits associated with a human mind such as learning and problem-solving.

Machine learning which is a subset of AI feeds on data and uses statistical techniques to help it "learn" how to get progressively better at a task, without having been specifically programmed for that task. With big data being part of the IoT architecture, Artificial Intelligence has become quite powerful in the IoT context.

Devices as part of the IoT ecosystem generate huge amounts of data. With big data, we have data lakes which store petabytes of data. The key aspect is to understand how we use this data and make best use of it. This is where Artificial Intelligence comes into play, where AI can perform a lot of functions such as anomaly detection, root cause analysis, and so on.

AI fits in very well in the context of industrial automation and predictive maintenance. In the old and traditional IoT implementations, the architecture had a rules engine that performs repetitive tasks, such as if a sensor data hits a defined threshold, it does a specific predefined task. As an example, if the temperature of a furnace goes beyond 70 degree Celsius, it shuts down the furnace. However, all these rules and values are hardcoded. With the introduction of AI in the IoT architecture, instead of having these rules hardcoded, enterprises can now deploy a model and get systems trained over a period of time, so that there is no hardcoding of business logic or rules. With AI, we are letting the machine learn from the patterns over a period of time so that actions can be performed based on the learnings. This helps in several use cases such as predictive maintenance. For example, we deployed an IoT-based predictive maintenance solution for a large car manufacturer that predicts spindle damages as well as identifies cracking and spalling of rotating equipment, gearing, and motor defects. As a result, they improved the Overall Equipment Effectiveness (OEE) by reducing diagnostic times by up to 70% and repair times by more than 20%. This adds a lot of value to enterprises.

One challenge that I have faced with AI in IoT is that there is a lot of data that needs to be sent to the cloud, and in many industries, the time it takes to execute a command based on the AI algorithms is too long since data needs to be transferred back and forth to the cloud for machines to learn from data. The other challenge which I have encountered is that a few enterprises from regulated industries consider data to be sensitive to be sent to the cloud. To overcome this challenge, enterprises need AI algorithms to be executed near to the devices where data is being generated. This means that such tasks need to be performed by the Smart IoT Gateways, which is also called AI at the edge. But not all Smart Gateways will have such compute power to run AI algorithms on the edge. There are several enterprises that have come up with Smart IoT Gateways which are capable of running AI algorithms near to the devices.

There are different models that enterprises adopt to enable AI in an IoT architecture. In some cases, AI is performed directly by Smart IoT Gateways using the data from the devices called AI on the edge. In some cases where enormous data is pumped from the devices, part of the AI happens at the Smart IoT Gateway level and the rest at the Full Stack IoT Platform level, and in some cases enterprises choose to perform AI at the Full Stack IoT Platform level. Enterprises need to choose the best place to perform AI based on the data and the use cases it is implementing. For one of the manufacturing companies, we used Amazon AWS Snowball Edge to perform heavy compute operations near to the IoT devices, that is, Smart IoT Gateway. Snowball Edge is capable of running a full-blown machine learning model at the IoT Gateway. The way this works is that you train the model in the public cloud, and then you bring the model to the IoT Gateway and run it. And when it detects that the predictions are not very accurate, it goes back to the data lake which is hosted at the Full Stack IoT Platform level to get further trained and again gets deployed to the IoT Gateway, and this cycle continues until the algorithm is performing actions with 100% accuracy.

With AI and machine learning in IoT, the static rules engine is replaced with dynamic and machine learning rules which means that reactive maintenance is replaced with predictive maintenance.

The whole convergence of IoT and Artificial Intelligence is opening a lot of avenues for excellence in IoT. For example, when we get into connected cars, the connected car is literally an edge computing on wheels. It has a lot of compute power that is actually processing the data as it comes in. And that is one classic example of edge computing on wheels and similarly aircrafts run edge computing and a lot of vehicles will run and industrial equipment will in future.

Typical Activities Performed by the Smart IoT Gateway and Full Stack IoT Platform

We discussed about the importance of Smart IoT Gateways and the Full Stack IoT Platform. Vendors have developed products in these two areas with several similarities in functionality, and many times these products perform the same activities as the other. Therefore, it becomes very confusing for enterprises to decide which process needs to be performed at which layer. The following is a typical guide that splits the responsibilities between the Smart IoT Gateway and the Full Stack IoT Platform.

Smart IoT Gateway	Full Stack IoT Platform
Basic data visualization	Complex analytics
Basic data analytics and short-term data historian features	Big data mining
Data caching, buffering, and streaming	Sources of business logic
Data preprocessing, cleansing, filtering, and optimization	Machine learning rules
Some data aggregation	Advanced visualizations
Device-to-device communications/M2M	Long-term data storage/ warehousing
Artificial Intelligence (Edge AI)	Artificial Intelligence

Security

Security in an IoT environment needs to be looked at across all the three layers within the IoT Standards Reference Model – the first is security at the device level, second is security at the Smart Gateway level, and third at the IoT Platform level. Apart from security at the hardware and software

77

level within these three layers, security at the network level becomes of the utmost importance and needs to be foolproof since communications between the three layers in an IoT Standards Reference Model happen over the Internet.

IoT security has become the subject of scrutiny after a number of high-profile incidents where a common IoT device was used to infiltrate and attack the larger network. Implementing security measures is critical to ensuring the safety of networks and IoT devices connected to them.

We are going to discuss the role of a security advisor in Chapter 13, as part of the IoT core team. This role needs to ensure that the right devices, platforms, Gateways, and networks are chosen that satisfy the security postures of an enterprise. In an IoT environment, device, Gateway, and platform security is the most important aspect to consider apart from application security.

Device Security

On the device side of security in an IoT ecosystem, enterprises need to ensure that they deploy devices in their OT estate which have security built into the device, and this is a must. Not only security needs to be built into the device but there should be a way to fix any security issues as they come up via software updates or upgrades.

One issue related to traditional IoT devices is that they are often resource constrained and do not contain the compute resources necessary to implement strong security. As such, many devices do not offer advanced security features. For example, most sensors that monitor humidity or temperature cannot handle advanced encryption or other security measures. Traditionally, numerous IoT devices are built to be placed in the field or on a machine and left until end of life, and they hardly ever receive security updates or patches. Therefore, from some enterprise's viewpoint, building security from the start can be costly and would slow down development. However, for enterprises aspiring to adopt IoT for their business, building security in the devices is a must. However, the level of security required in devices also depends on the use cases and industry. As an example, a hacker will be less interested to break into an agriculture IoT device and more keen to break into a manufacturing plant.

Enterprises also need to make sure that access to the devices and all the data that is produced through these devices is controlled by the authorized users or systems. And any data that are stored on the devices or transmitted across the communication pathways are all encrypted and secure.

Smart IoT Gateway Security

Gateways are an important part of an IoT ecosystem but are a vulnerable, single point of hackability. IoT Gateways are often the first ones to be attacked because they have higher processing power for running more intensive applications. More power means better software, and better software means more vulnerabilities for a hacker to exploit. Another key reason why IoT Gateways become a hotspot for many hackers is because of its location as an edge device between the Internet and the intranet. The Gateway is typically the first point of entry for any security threat (as well as a system's first line of defense).

There are many matured IoT Gateways that are existing in the market, and a careful selection needs to be made, keeping security in mind. Some factors to be considered while making an IoT Gateway selection are listed in the following.

Message security: An IoT Gateway needs to have strong end-to-end encryption methodologies. Messages should be encrypted and can only be decrypted by the recipient using cryptographic keys. This allows a Gateway device to still accept and pass on data, but it will not be able to read the data. Thus, in the case of a security compromise, the hacker will not be able to parse and read the data from the Gateway device.

Device onboarding security: Device onboarding occurs when a new device is added within the IoT ecosystem. Key management practices, and how keys are exchanged when new devices are accepted, are a large security vulnerability. Physical tampering can also lead to private keys being extracted. It is important to understand how the Gateway manufacturer handles security at the device onboarding level.

Integration security: IoT API security is an important consideration. IoT systems transmit and receive large volumes of data and information, and it is important to be able to have secure data movement between devices, Gateways, and back-end databases. Because integrations are vulnerable, one must continuously scan and test to ensure integrity of data within the system.

Over-the-air security updates: Firmware updates need to happen within an IoT ecosystem, and it is necessary to understand how these updates are taking place and how an IoT Gateway is handling them securely.

IoT Platform Security

An IoT platform is the hub where all the IoT data resides and, in many cases, Device Management is performed, which is an important part of an IoT ecosystem. Security at an IoT Platform level is extremely important; however, the good news is that a lot has been done by different product vendors in this space on security. Almost all large platform vendors, such as Amazon, Microsoft, and Google, offer services for all layers of security including preventive security mechanisms like encryption and access control to device data along with services to continuously monitor and audit configurations.

Blockchain

Trust is the most critical component to a human exchange. Trust is always a key component and is the ability for one person to effectively deal with others and for enterprises to perform business and to build civilization as well. We traditionally have centralized institutions that manage the trust part for every transaction. As an example, in a money exchange transaction, since we do not trust unknown individuals or businesses, an intermediary, such as a bank which we trust, sits in the middle and coordinates payments for us. And this is a model that allows us to think about resolving the problem of trust so that we can confidently enter into exchange with others. However, intermediaries add a lot of friction and costs along with several transactional challenges. Blockchain technology is trying to solve this problem of trust in a much secure and cheaper way without anyone needing to depend on an intermediary. This is not only limited to banks but applies to public utilities and institutional controls where there is some form of exchange between parties.

A blockchain is a decentralized and distributed digital ledger consisting of records called blocks that is used to record transactions across many computers so that any involved block cannot be altered retroactively, without the alteration of all subsequent blocks. It is a distributed ledger technology (DLT) that allows data to be stored globally on thousands of servers while letting anyone on the network see everyone else's entries in near real time. That makes it difficult for one user to gain control or change the network.

Blockchain is a system of recording information in a way that makes it difficult or impossible to change or hack the system. A blockchain is essentially a digital ledger of transactions that is duplicated and distributed across the entire network of computer systems on the blockchain. Each block in the chain contains a number of transactions, and every time a new transaction occurs on the blockchain, a record of that transaction is added to every (participant's) ledger.

There is a lot of debate around blockchain trying to solve every marketplace problem, but blockchain is a technology that is tailored to address a few problems only. And in terms of costs, the fundamental thing which blockchain will address is reducing cost of transaction. As an example, person A wakes up and authenticates themselves, buys something online, and engages in some sort of digital transaction. Every such transaction needs to be verified, such as who is involved, the amounts exchanged, and so on, and the society spends a lot of resources and money to making sure that those attributes (transactions and actors) are correct and that transactions are executed without problems. Currently, there are several intermediaries as part of each such transaction. Blockchain is a technology that drastically reduces the cost to verify that a specific attribute is true and genuine.

In simple terms, blockchain is a new decentralized distributed way of managing information across parties who do not necessarily trust each other but have an interest in a common outcome.

As an example, a common outcome of a "farm to fork" process in a food chain starts from agricultural production to selling the product by the retailer to consumption by a consumer. In such a setup, there are different actors involved such as farmers who produce fruits and vegetables, freight management companies that transport these products from the farm to the stores using the right temperature-controlled fridges, retailers who sell these products, and consumers who buy and consume these products. Managing information across all these actors in a transparent and tamper-proof way is the most important element in this use case. The common outcome of this use case is that the consumers can trust the quality of the products and buy these products so that each actor in the supply chain makes profits, and this can be enabled with IoT and blockchain technology. This is the main reason why Blockchain has become an integral part of the IoT Standards Reference Model.

On one side, there are several examples where IoT has created tremendous value from blockchain, and there are opposite examples where blockchain has added a lot of value to IoT.

Let me explain this with a food safety case study. If you walk into a Walmart store and buy some fruits, as a consumer how do we currently determine the quality of the product? We just based our quality assumption on the trust we have on Walmart. We do not know who has produced the fruit and how much chemicals have been used during farming, whether the fruits have been transported using the right temperatures and within a certain timeframe, and where the fruits have been packed, tested, and processed. With blockchain and IoT, the entire sequence of steps from farm to fork can be made transparent to the customer without depending on any intermediaries, and therefore this can be considered a great technology to explore.

The key aspect in the case study is to determine how we ensure that that information that is getting into the blockchain is accurate and trusted. As long as there are humans that are sending information, such as the temperature in which a product is stored, data can be tampered. If it is coming from a tamper-proof endpoint, such as an IoT device sending the temperature information on a periodic basis to the blockchain, it adds much more trust to the blockchain-based traceability solution. This is one of the examples where IoT contributes tremendous value to blockchain-based solutions.

Another example where blockchain adds a lot of value to IoT is in the pharma industry. The pharmaceutical counterfeit drug problem is a $200 billion problem which can be addressed qualitatively with Blockchain and IoT. If all transactions starting from procuring raw materials to drug manufacturing till transporting and handing over the drug to the customer can be recorded using blockchain using a tamper-proof tag, the counterfeit issue can be addressed. With blockchain, besides traceability there is added trust since none of the transactions can be changed in the blockchain world.

Conversely, let us take an example of connected cars. We have heard about multiple cases where some third-party fraudsters figured out a way to break in the car while we are driving. In almost 70% of the cases, this is caused during a software upgrade where hackers try to gain entry into the car systems posing as genuine actors and take control of the systems. If such a coordination of software upgrades can be mediated through a blockchain, enterprises can ensure that the right actors who have the right permissions are the only ones who are able to send the transaction to the car systems apart from making sure that software that is sent is signed and is not tampered. Such an approach begins to see blockchain adding value to an IoT-based solution.

Blockchain resolves the fundamental element of trust. However, the core issue in an end-to-end transaction for any enterprise is that there are a variety of actors and enterprises with different interests that need to subscribe to the same blockchain model to complete a transaction, and it is not always mandatory that all of them will do so. If not all parties subscribe to the model from an industry perspective, enterprises will not get the full value of applying the technology. So it is really important that the manufacturers and the transportation companies and the retailers and the delivery companies subscribe to the model.

Assuming everyone subscribes to the mode, with so many actors to enable an end-to-end transaction, it is essential to understand who owns the data, who owns the business logic that runs on the blockchain, who can add new services on top of the existing blockchain, and who will decide who can join the network and who can leave the network. This brings in the most important element of blockchain governance which needs to be addressed while the blockchain solution is implemented in an IoT Standards Reference Model.

A public blockchain is permissionless. Anyone can join the network and read, write, or participate within the blockchain. A public blockchain is decentralized and does not have a single entity which controls the network. Data on a public blockchain are secure as it is not possible to modify or alter data once they have been validated on the blockchain.

A private blockchain is a permissioned blockchain. Private blockchains work based on access controls which restrict the people who can participate in the network. There are one or more entities which control the network, and this leads to reliance on third parties to transact. In a private blockchain, only the entities participating in a transaction will have knowledge about it, whereas the others will not be able to access it.

A combination of IoT and Blockchain enables end-to-end business insights with complete security. However, it is essential to note that as part of the IoT landscape, a private blockchain is best suited since IoT is industry- and enterprise-centric, and the general public is not allowed to be part of this initiative.

Summary

In this chapter, we discussed about the IoT Standards Reference Model, which is broadly split into three horizontal services and two vertical services.

The horizontal services are the Full Stack IoT Platform, Smart IoT Gateway, and Devices:

- The device layer is where the physical objects are located on the shop floors.

- The Smart IoT Gateway is responsible for collecting data from devices and relaying it to the rest of the systems. In many scenarios, the Smart IoT Gateway performs the preprocessing of the data collected from devices including analytics. Another feature the Smart IoT Gateway performs is Device Management. Some enterprises choose to perform Device Management at the Smart IoT Gateway level, but others prefer to perform Device Management in the next block which is at the Full Stack IoT Platform level.

- The Full Stack IoT Platform is where the IoT data coming from devices via the Smart IoT Gateway is combined with other non-IoT data to derive useful insights using analytics systems or applications.

The two vertical services are Blockchain and security:

- Though Blockchain is currently evolving in the context of IoT, it is quite essential that enterprises plan this function while deciding their IoT architecture as Blockchain is going to become the most important element for enterprises to succeed with IoT in the future.

- The devices, Smart IoT Gateways, and Full Stack IoT Platform need to be secured, which is one of the key implicit requirements of the IoT Standards Reference Model.

In the next chapter, we will discuss about the different IoT devices and their communication protocols, including their limitations and challenges.

CHAPTER 5

IoT Devices and Their Communication

IoT devices are the nonstandard computing devices that connect wirelessly to a network and have the ability to transmit data. IoT involves extending Internet connectivity beyond standard devices, such as desktops, laptops, smartphones, and tablets, to non-Internet-enabled physical devices and everyday objects. Embedded with technology, these devices can communicate and interact over the Internet. They can also be remotely monitored and controlled.

IoT devices, also called connected devices, talk to other related devices in an environment to automate home and industry tasks. Devices are typically categorized into three main groups: consumer, enterprise, and industrial.

Consumer-connected devices include smart TVs, smart speakers, toys, wearables, and smart appliances. Smart meters, commercial security systems, smart city technologies, and manufacturing automation are examples of industrial and enterprise IoT devices. Other technologies, including smart air conditioning, smart thermostats, smart lighting, and smart security, span across home, enterprise, and industrial uses.

In a smart home, for example, once a user arrives home, their car communicates with the garage to open the door. Once inside the home, the thermostat is already adjusted to their preferred temperature, and

© Venkatesh Upadrista 2021
V. Upadrista, *IoT Standards with Blockchain*,
https://doi.org/10.1007/978-1-4842-7271-8_5

the lighting is set to a lower intensity and color, as their pacemaker data indicates it has been a stressful day.

In the enterprise, smart sensors located in a conference room can help an employee locate and schedule an available room for a meeting, ensuring the proper room type, size, and features are available. When meeting attendees enter the room, the temperature will adjust according to the occupancy, the lights will dim as the appropriate PowerPoint loads on the screen, and the speaker can directly begin their presentation.

On a plant floor, an assembly line machine fitted with sensors will provide sensor data to the plant operator, informing them of anomalies and predicting when parts will need to be replaced. Such information can prevent unexpected downtime, along with lost productivity and profits.

There are several such use cases for every industry, and the IoT market is gaining a lot of popularity. IoT has already provided rise to several applications that are used by businesses, including factory automation, smart cities, smart homes, connected cars, and ehealth.

The adoption of IoT across enterprises is increasing at a very fast pace; however, challenges are also enormous. One such challenge the IoT industry is facing is with device connectivity. Device connectivity is one of the biggest challenges in an IoT implementation, and this is because there are several legacy devices that an IoT ecosystem needs to integrate, and each one operates using different and unique wired and wireless protocols. IoT devices are split into three categories, which are discussed in the following.

Device Types

Figure 5-1 depicts the three types of IoT devices that exist in an IoT ecosystem. The first type of devices is the small things, the second is called the big things, and the third is the complex things.

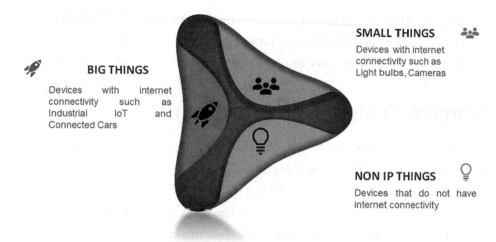

SMALL THINGS

Devices with internet connectivity such as Light bulbs, Cameras

BIG THINGS

Devices with internet connectivity such as Industrial IoT and Connected Cars

NON IP THINGS

Devices that do not have internet connectivity

Figure 5-1. *Types of devices*

Small Things (Type 1 Devices)

Small things, also called type 1 devices, are things which are connectable to the Internet, such as devices with small sensors. These devices have smaller memory, and they consume minimal power and Internet bandwidth and many times are connected over a SIM card. Their data model is simple, and most of the times they operate on batteries.

An example of small things is the smart light bulb and smart door locks. A smart light bulb does not have thousands of parameters to control. There is on and off and dimming functionality, and in some cases, a bulb may send data on how much power is being consumed.

Big Things (Type 2 Devices)

Big things could be something such as heavy machinery or industrial IoT connected cars. These are devices that have enough power supply, ample Internet connectivity, and in most cases are able to connect to the Internet. Though these devices have all the required features to connect to an IoT network, the data model is very complex, and it constitutes of thousands of parameters to be controlled. These parameters range from making complex decisions based on a certain event and executing some complex algorithms.

Complex Things (Type 3 Devices)

The third and most interesting devices are type 3 devices which are called the complex things. Complex things, though called IoT devices, are not really IoT because they do not have the Internet (I from the IoT) part in them. These are devices such as Philips Hue, Amazon Echo Plus (with Alexa for voice controls), and Honeywell thermostats. Type 3 devices communicate using non-Internet-enabled protocols, such as Zigbee and Z-Wave, and therefore they cannot connect to the Internet. However, in the IoT world, it is essential that all devices, irrespective of their type, connect to the Internet. Most enterprises in manufacturing or medical industries will have several complex things in their ecosystem. The more complex things existing in an enterprise, the more difficult it becomes for IoT implementation in these enterprises.

Communication Protocols

The communication protocols in the IoT world are classified into seven broad standards, which are described in the following. Each standard has its own benefits and challenges and is applicable to specific use cases and industries.

LPWAN (Low-Power Wide Area Network)

LPWAN is a protocol which provides long-range communication on small and inexpensive batteries that last for years. This family of technologies is purpose-built to support large-scale IoT networks sprawling over vast industrial and commercial campuses.

LPWANs can connect all types of IoT sensors – facilitating numerous applications from asset tracking, environmental monitoring, and facility management to occupancy detection and consumables monitoring.

The drawback with LPWAN is that it can only send small blocks of data at a low rate, and therefore devices using LPWAN connectivity are better suited for use cases that do not require high bandwidth and are not time sensitive.

LPWAN is used for different applications, such as smart metering, smart parking, smart grid control, smart security, smart city, smart agriculture, asset tracking, smart home automation, critical infrastructure monitoring, personal IoT applications, logistics, and so on.

LPWAN has two variants, namely, licensed and unlicensed. The licensed version of LPWAN runs on public cellular networks and can be operated and managed by several telecom mobile operators. It supports roaming and hence there is no issue of interoperability apart from being secure and reliable as it uses exclusive frequency per connection.

The unlicensed version of LPWAN uses unlicensed frequency spectrum and does not use exclusive frequency for each connection and can be used by anyone without any exclusivity. This means that the unlicensed spectrum may lead to interference among devices using the same radio spectrum and cannot be used for high-speed connections. Unlicensed LPWAN technologies include LoRaWAN, Sigfox, etc.

Satellite Communications Networks (3G/4G/5G)

Satellite communications enable cellphone communications from devices such as phones to the next antenna of about 10–15 miles. In the Internet of Things language, this form of communication is mostly referred to as "M2M" (machine-to-machine) because it allows devices such as a phone to send and receive data through the cell network. Satellite communications networks offer reliable broadband communication supporting various voice calls and video streaming applications. On the downside, they impose very high operational costs and power requirements.

While cellular networks are not viable for the majority of IoT applications powered by battery-operated sensor networks, they fit well in specific Industrial IoT use cases such as in manufacturing plants, connected cars, or fleet management in transportation and logistics.

For example, in-car infotainment, traffic routing, advanced driver assistance systems (ADAS) alongside fleet telematics and tracking services can all rely on high bandwidth cellular connectivity.

Cellular next-generation 5G with high-speed mobility support and ultra-low latency is positioned to be the future of autonomous vehicles and augmented reality. 5G is also expected to enable real-time video surveillance for public safety, real-time mobile delivery of medical data sets for connected health, and several time-sensitive industrial automation applications in the future.

A mesh topology is a network setup where each computer and network device is interconnected with one another. This topology setup allows for most transmissions to be distributed even if one of the connections goes down. It is a topology commonly used for wireless networks. Infotainment, also called soft news, is a type of media, usually television, that provides a combination of information and entertainment.

Radio Frequency (RF) Networks

Radio frequency communications are probably the easiest form of communications between devices. Protocols like Zigbee or Z-Wave use a low-power RF radio embedded or retrofitted into electronic devices and systems.

Zigbee is a short-range, low-power, wireless standard. Compared to LPWAN, Zigbee provides higher data rates, but at the same time much less power efficiency.

Because of their physical short range, Zigbee and similar protocols such as Z-Wave, Thread, etc. are best suited for medium-range IoT applications with an even distribution of nodes in close proximity. Typically, Zigbee is suitable for various home automation use cases like smart lighting, HVAC (Heating, Ventilation, and Air Conditioning) controls, security, and energy management, leveraging home sensor networks.

Bluetooth

Bluetooth is a wireless technology standard used for exchanging data between fixed and mobile devices over short distances.

Bluetooth Classic was originally intended for point-to-point or point-to-multipoint data exchange among consumer devices. Optimized for power consumption, Bluetooth Low Energy (BLE) was later introduced to address small-scale consumer IoT applications.

BLE-enabled devices are mostly used in conjunction with electronic devices, typically smartphones that serve as a hub for transferring data to the cloud. Nowadays, BLE is widely integrated into fitness and medical wearables (e.g., smartwatches, glucose meters, pulse oximeters, etc.) as well as smart home devices (e.g., door locks), whereby data is conveniently communicated to and visualized on smartphones.

Beacons are small, wireless transmitters that use low-energy Bluetooth technology to send signals to other smart devices nearby. Put simply, they connect and transmit information to smart devices, making location-based searching and interaction easier and more accurate.

The release of new specifications called Bluetooth Mesh in 2017 aimed to enable a more scalable deployment of BLE devices, particularly in retail contexts. BLE beacons have been used to unlock new service innovations like in-store navigation, personalized promotions, and content delivery.

Wi-Fi

Wi-Fi is a wireless local area network (WLAN) that provides Internet access to devices that are within the range (about 66 feet from the access point).

In the IoT space, Wi-Fi's major limitations in coverage, scalability, and power consumption make the technology much less prevalent. Imposing high energy requirements, Wi-Fi is often not a feasible solution for large networks of battery-operated IoT sensors, especially in industrial IoT and smart building scenarios. Instead, it more pertains to connecting devices that can be conveniently connected to a power outlet like smart home gadgets and appliances, digital signages, or security cameras.

Wi-Fi 6 is the newest Wi-Fi generation and brings in greatly enhanced network bandwidth to improve data throughput per user in congested environments. The Wi-Fi 6 standard is transforming customer experience with new digital mobile services in retail and mass entertainment sectors. Also, in-car networks for infotainment and onboard diagnostics are expected to be the most game-changing use cases for Wi-Fi 6.

RFID

Radio Frequency Identification (RFID) uses radio waves to transmit small amounts of data from an RFID tag to a reader within a very short distance. Till now, the technology has facilitated a major revolution in retail and logistics.

By attaching an RFID tag to products and equipment, businesses can track their inventory and assets in real time, allowing for better stock and production planning as well as optimized supply chain management. Alongside increasing IoT adoption, RFID continues to be entrenched in the retail sector, enabling new IoT applications like smart shelves, self-checkout, and smart mirrors.

The Wired Networks

A wired network uses an Ethernet cable to connect to the network. The Ethernet cable is in turn connected to a Digital Subscriber Line (DSL) or to the Internet Gateway. The wired networks are mature technology, and it is easy to get plugged into since enterprises already have phone lines, power lines, and coaxial cable lines.

Even in the case of wireless networks, those networks are usually connected to a wired network at some point; hence, the most commonly used network is a hybrid of both wired and wireless network connectivity.

As an example, PROFINET is one of the industry technical standards for data communication over Industrial Ethernet, designed for collecting data from and controlling equipment in industrial systems. PROFINET is based on standard Ethernet and can connect seamlessly with any wireless standard such as WLAN or Bluetooth.

Another example is the Modbus protocol. Modbus is a serial communication protocol for use with programmable logic controllers (PLCs). PLCs are used in manufacturing processes and are typically used to transmit signals from instrumentation and control devices back to a main controller or data gathering system, for example, a system that measures temperature and humidity and communicates the results to a computer.

DSL is a type of connection that transmits data over a telephone network through a telephone cable.

Coax, short for coaxial, is a type of cable used to transmit data, the Internet, video, and voice communications.

A programmable logic controller or programmable controller is an industrial digital computer that has been ruggedized and adapted for the control of manufacturing processes, such as assembly lines, robotic devices, or any activity that requires high reliability, ease of programming, and process fault diagnosis.

Choosing the Right Smart IoT Gateway for Industry Use Cases

Each industry vertical has its own unique set of network requirements. Smart IoT Gateways connect devices to other layers within the IoT Standards Reference Model, and therefore choosing the right Smart IoT Gateway means accurately weighing criteria in terms of what type of devices are used within that specific industry domain and then getting down into the specifics of what devices the enterprise is looking to connect for their specific use cases. Table 5-1 provides a view on the communication protocols most widely used across industries.

Table 5-1. *Protocols Vs Industry Specific Use Cases*

IoT Verticals	LPWAN	Satellite Networks	RFID	Radio Networks	Bluetooth BLE	Wi-Fi	Wired
Industrial IoT	▶	▷		▷			▶
Smart meter	▶						▶
Smart city	▶						▷
Smart building	▶				▷		▷
Smart home			▶		▶	▶	

(*continued*)

Table 5-1. (*continued*)

IoT Verticals	LPWAN	Satellite Networks	RFID	Radio Networks	Bluetooth BLE	Wi-Fi	Wired
Wearables	▷				►		
Connected car						▷	
Connected health	►				►		▷
Smart retail		▷	►		►	▷	
Logistics and asset tracking	▷	►	►				
Smart agriculture	►						

▷ *Moderately applicable* ► *Highly applicable*

For one of the industrial equipment manufacturing companies called Company A, we deployed Edge Gateway 5000 from Dell as their Smart IoT Gateway. Company A's requirement was to place their Smart IoT Gateway at a location that can withstand high temperature and higher levels of humidity and should be able to operate 24/7. On the other side, being a manufacturing company, there were several devices that the Smart IoT Gateway needs to connect, such as their PLC systems (which run on Modbus), apart from connecting to devices that were using Zigbee and 6LoWPAN protocols. Based on this need, Edge Gateway 5000 was selected for this enterprise.

KEY POINTS

- Small things, also called type 1 devices, are things which are connectable to the Internet, such as devices with small sensors.

- Big things could be something such as heavy machinery or industrial IoT connected cars. These are devices that have enough power supply, ample Internet connectivity, and in most cases are able to connect to the Internet.

- Complex things, though called IoT devices, are not really IoT because they do not have the Internet (I from the IoT) part in them.

Summary

In this chapter, we discussed about the three types of devices, which are called the small things which are simple Internet-enabled devices, the big things such as heavy machinery, and complex things which are devices that are not Internet enabled.

- Small things, also called type 1 devices, are things which are connectable to the Internet, such as devices with small sensors.

- Big things could be something such as heavy machinery or industrial IoT connected cars. These are devices that have enough power supply, ample Internet connectivity, and in most cases are able to connect to the Internet.

- Complex things, though called IoT devices, are not really IoT because they do not have the Internet (I from the IoT) part in them.

We then discussed about the different communication protocols that these devices use along with a guidance on which Smart IoT Gateway to choose based on the devices that need to connect with the IoT ecosystem.

In the next chapter, we will discuss about the Smart IoT Gateway, which is a system to connect multiple devices (using varied protocols) to the IoT ecosystem.

CHAPTER 6

The Smart IoT Gateway

Organizations implementing IoT are increasingly focusing on the business outcomes using technology, and IoT initiatives are no longer being driven by the sole purpose of internal operational improvement. IT and business stakeholders are working together to align IoT projects with business outcomes for improving revenue and customer experience, but they are facing challenges because of the legacy systems and approaches. Legacy is not going to go away, and this is the fact, but there are enablers that are helping enterprises in overcoming these challenges – the Smart IoT Gateway is one such enabler.

Tech analyst company IDC predicts that in total there will be 41.6 billion connected IoT devices by 2025, or "things." It also suggests industrial and automotive equipment represent the largest opportunity of connected "things," but it also sees a strong adoption of smart home and wearable devices in the near term. Another tech analyst, Gartner,[1] predicts that the enterprise and automotive sectors will account for 5.8 billion devices this year, up almost a quarter in 2019. Utilities will be the highest user of IoT with the rollout of smart meters. Security devices, in the form of intruder detection and web cameras, will be the second biggest use case of

---

[1] www.gartner.com/en/newsroom/press-releases/2019-08-29-gartner-says-5-8-billion-enterprise-and-automotive-io

© Venkatesh Upadrista 2021
V. Upadrista, *IoT Standards with Blockchain*,
https://doi.org/10.1007/978-1-4842-7271-8_6

IoT devices. Building automation like connected lighting will be the fastest growing sector, followed by automotive (connected cars) and healthcare (monitoring of chronic conditions). This is a clear indication that though there are numerous challenges enterprises are facing, IoT is going to be the future for enterprises to do business, and organizations with high levels of IoT maturity achieve higher rates of success in their IoT adoption.

IoT is all about making life and work easier and trustworthy for individuals and enterprises – it could be about securing home using home security devices or automatically switching the air conditioning and heating units in a large building, or it could be about predictive maintenance to reduce the downtime in factories. In a mining industry, IoT can help avoid sending technicians on a truck or a helicopter every month to go and see if an equipment is working fine. With IoT, enterprises can predict the cycles of breakage and technicians can reach the mining spots when there is a real maintenance required because an equipment is about to break in the next one- or two-week time. This not only saves cost for enterprises but enables them to become much more efficient.

In an IoT world, there are two departments that need to come along which traditionally and culturally have not spent a lot of time together so far – these are the Information Technology (IT) and the Operational Technology (OT) departments. A typical IT department is measured on system uptime, availability of applications and IT infrastructure, number of security breaches, and reducing costs of IT. On the other side, the OT department constitutes of the factory managers, production managers, and even agriculture farmers. These are the folks who produce food, control the oil and gas process, pump oil from the ground, or are folks who are responsible for maintaining the fleet of the company trucks. An OT department is measured on entirely different success criteria, such as what is the yield of the crop, how much water is being used to create that yield, what is the production uptime of the factory, what is being done to save fuel in a fleet of hundreds of trucks, how can safety of drivers be increased, how to stop people from stealing the contents out of the trucks or stores, and so on.

IT and OT departments are two different worlds, and each department is measured very different on success. With IoT, both these departments need to come together, and this is where connecting people becomes equally important along with connecting things. In an IoT world, both IT and OT absolutely have to come together to be able to work on these projects, and then enterprises also need to bring in support functions, such as finance, marketing, and sales departments, and all of these departments together will be able to make best-of-breed IoT solutions. This is one of the major aspects among several others that enterprises need to address before embarking on an IoT journey at the enterprise level.

A few years back when there were discussions around IoT, experts used to explain about the basics of IoT and its associated benefits. On the other side, there were enterprises where IT and OT staff were meeting for the first time. Fast forward to today, it would be very rare for an IoT discussion to start where one needs to explain about the basics of IoT, and secondly we see more and more synergies coming together between IT and OT teams.

However, the barriers are still high, and there are still several challenges for enterprises embarking on an IoT journey. The top six challenges which enterprises need to address in an enterprise-wide IoT implementation are described in Figure 6-1.[2]

---

[2] The Art of Consultative Selling in IT: Taking Blue Ocean Strategy a Step Ahead Hardcover – 29 Jun. 2017 by Venkatesh Upadrista

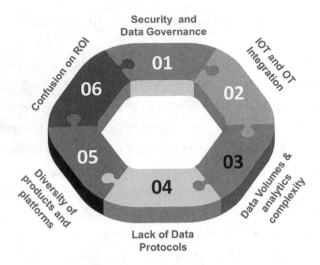

Figure 6-1. *IoT challenges*

Security

The first challenge that is always on the top priority for every enterprise in an IoT context is security. As part of the IoT implementation, enterprises are exposing devices (things) such as machinery and sensors to the Internet, which primarily were not designed for Internet-enabled communications, and hence cyber security was never thought about in these devices. We are trying to make each and every device within an Operational Technology world accessible over the Internet, which means we have opened the surface area of attack incredibly wide. Though a lot has been done in this area, security still remains the number one challenge. We are going to discuss in detail about security and how to address this concern in Chapter 8.

IT-OT Team Integration

The second challenge is bringing IT and OT staff together to achieve the IoT vision. Though this team is coming together lately, it is very essential for enterprises to make sure that this team is fully aligned on one single objective to make the IoT use case successful. We will discuss about the IoT core team in Chapter 13 and try to address this challenge.

Data Volume and Analytics

The third major barrier is the data volume and analytics complexity. The surge of IoT data comes with a lot of economic value, estimated at around $11 trillion by 2025. But it also comes with some significant challenges due to huge volumes of data, which make data aggregation and data analytics complex. This leads to difficulties in quickly and easily extracting strategic value from IoT use cases.

The primary challenge of IoT data is its real-time nature. According to IDC[3], by 2025, 30% of all data will be real time, with IoT accounting for nearly 95% of it, 20% of all data will be critical, and 10% of all data will be hypercritical. Analytics will have to happen in real time for companies to benefit from these types of data. Though it is clear that IoT generates an enormous amount of data, this is not the main challenge. The key issue is that not many enterprises have a data-driven culture – what this means is that enterprises have still not created a mature process to manage big data in their enterprise. The challenge is not about the data volumes, but it is more about where do I get the data, how I stitch the data together to make meaningful insights, how do I manage and maintain this data, and how do I do this in the most appropriate way. Chapter 11 will discuss about the

---

[3]www.zdnet.com/article/by-2025-nearly-30-percent-of-data-generated-will-be-real-time-idc-says/

big data platform that will help ensure that the right platform and tools are chosen to manage and govern data meaningfully.

Lack of Standard Communication (Data) Protocols

The fourth challenge comes from the fact that there are enormous legacy devices within an enterprise, and each device has its own protocols that make communication between the different layers of an IoT Standards Reference Model very difficult. We will discuss in subsequent chapters how IoT Gateways can solve this challenge.

Diversity of Products and Platforms

The fifth major challenge is the diversified products and platforms that form the complete IoT ecosystem. If any vendor or service provider says that they can deploy an end-to-end IoT solution without requiring any partner ecosystem, then there is something fundamentally wrong with their solution. An IoT solution requires a huge ecosystem starting from device vendors to IoT Gateway manufacturers to IoT Cloud providers that makes the complete solution, and enterprises need to look at the best-of-breed solution in each of these areas that can make the whole solution cost-effective and efficient.

Return on Investment

The final challenge that is coming up lately is on return on investments. The discussion in an IoT context within an enterprise has moved away from an IT level (Chief Information Officer level) to a finance level (Chief Financial Officer level), and there are clear asks from the CFO on the return on investments for an IoT implementation, which needs to be clearly thought of and articulated. After all, IoT will require the CAPEX investment followed by the OPEX investment.

Capital expenditures (CAPEX) are long-term expenses, while operating expenses (OPEX) are a company's day-to-day expenses. CAPEX typically are costs required at the start of any project, while in OPEX costs are spread across the project duration.

A data center is a building, a dedicated space within a building, or a group of buildings used to house computer systems and associated components within the enterprise premises. It is a network of computing and storage resources connected using local networks, enabling the delivery of shared software applications and data.

A cloud data service (referred to as a cloud service or cloud) is a remote version of a data center, located somewhere away from your company's physical premises, that lets enterprises access their data through the Internet. A data center traditionally refers to server hardware on your premises to store and access data through your local network.

Each of the challenges discussed earlier needs to be analyzed carefully while an enterprise embarks on their IoT journey. Apart from these challenges, enterprises need to understand that there is no single architecture that they can use as a guide toward an IoT implementation. Enterprises need to tailor their IoT architecture based on who they are (i.e., the industry they are in), what they do (i.e., manufacture products, create medicines, or sell groceries), what and how they are trying to connect things, and all these are massive dependencies that determine an IoT architecture.

There are multiple devices which enterprises need to connect in an IoT ecosystem, and these are devices which they do not manufacture. But if you look at the diversity of these devices on the field, one can easily understand these are devices that communicate using multiple different protocols, leading to a very complex IoT ecosystem. Most of the challenges we discussed so far can be addressed by bringing in a (Smart) IoT Gateway into the IoT Standards Reference Model.

IoT Gateways

There is a lot of complexity with devices and their protocols. As discussed in Chapter 5, devices use several protocols, such as Zigbee, Z-Wave, Wi-Fi, Bluetooth, and so on. On the other hand, there are several standard bodies and consortia that are all creating new standards and new protocols on a daily basis. This is where IoT Gateways come into the picture.

An IoT Gateway is a solution for enabling IoT communications, usually device-to-device communications or device-to-cloud communications. At its simplest form, a traditional IoT Gateway is a piece of hardware or software to collect and aggregate data from multiple I/O devices using multiple communication protocols. The Gateway then communicates the data to servers either in local data centers or in the cloud. In such a simplified context, the Gateway functions as a "broker." In this context, the Gateway either directly connects to IoT field equipment (sensors, actuators, etc.) or through programmable logic controllers (PLCs) or supervisory control and data acquisition systems (SCADA) which aggregate field data. These Gateways support a wide variety of I/O interfaces, including wired and wireless connections.

In such scenarios, Gateways serve two main objectives:

1. Allow more devices to connect to the Internet at an industrial scale

2. Support disparate protocols – from Zigbee to Wi-Fi to 4G/5G

A programmable logic controller or programmable controller is an industrial digital computer that has been ruggedized and adapted for the control of manufacturing processes, such as assembly lines, robotic devices, or any activity that requires high reliability, ease of programming, and process fault diagnosis.

Supervisory control and data acquisition (SCADA) is a control system architecture comprising computers, networked data communications, and graphical user interfaces (GUI) for high-level process supervisory management.

However, in a marketplace where Gartner expects 20 billion IoT devices to go live by 2020, a traditional Gateway has a lot of challenges because if all data needs to be sent from IoT devices to the cloud or data center, we are talking about a significant amount of data per second which in some use cases can range from a few terabytes to even petabytes of data transfer per minute. There is an enormous amount of raw data that IoT devices generate, and if this data is directly sent from IoT Gateways to the cloud, it introduces a lot of inefficiencies because data transfer from a device to the cloud causes latency and high costs and also can many times clog the network connectivity apart from inducing data privacy issues in some cases. So though Gateways are built to connect the unconnected, the other main task Gateways are expected to perform is to start the analytics process at the Gateway level. This is where edge computing has disrupted the market.

Edge computing is a distributed computing model that brings computation and data storage closer to the location where it is needed, to improve response times and save bandwidth. In edge computing, critical data processing occurs at the data source rather than in a centralized cloud-based location. Edge computing resolves the challenge of inefficient data transfer architecture by performing important tasks at the IoT Gateway itself. Gateways built using edge computing techniques are called Smart IoT Gateways.

So in essence on the OT side as we speak more about Smart IoT Gateways, it is really about managing millions of devices as easily as managing one thing apart from consuming all data from the devices, deriving insights, and then performing actions based on the insights. With Smart IoT Gateways, it is all about managing perishable data at the edge and only moving to the IoT Cloud platform data what is actually needed to store from a long-term perspective or to perform analytics on a very specialized data.

Smart IoT Gateways

One of the reasons why edge computing has gained prominence is because it can avoid high latency and sometimes can even reduce costs of storage.

There are use cases that deal with the life and death of individuals, such as in healthcare, and in such use cases, people's lives, safety, and high finances are at stake. These are examples where enterprises look at almost near to zero latency, and therefore there is no appetite to pass all the data back to the cloud for processing. Enterprises need to process data right at the source as quickly as possible by using Smart IoT Gateways. Smart IoT

Gateways should be capable of giving the same type of high power and performance and low latency that we would traditionally expect from IoT Platforms in the cloud or a data center.

Smart IoT Gateways should be able to perform the tasks to manage OT from the outside and IT from the inside. What this means is that there are different types of devices that enterprises deal with in an IoT use case, and every industry uses different devices. Devices used in building management are very different from those used in an automotive industry or in a pharmaceutical setting. These devices use multiple protocols and inputs/outputs, and they are going to be there with us for the next many years. It is essential that IoT solutions coexist with these devices and protocols. What this means is that Smart IoT Gateways should be capable of supporting and communicating with the magnitude of such OT devices so that enterprises can retrieve all data from these devices – so the first feature expected from Smart IoT Gateways is the ability to have the right connectivity to be able to connect and communicate with any type of device.

The second aspect is that these Smart IoT Gateways are not going to sit in the data centers or under desks or home environment. These are devices which will need to be very rugged as they may have to sit in windmills or boiler rooms under high temperatures, which are not a very easy environment to be, and at the same time, they have to last a long time and have to operate efficiently under these conditions. Often, Gateways become a mission-critical piece of an IoT architecture since most enterprises using IoT will depend on the devices to predict the future, so any downtime with these Gateways can lead to a business problem.

So in summary, when enterprises are shortlisting IoT Gateways, they need to first look at the protocols Gateways support based on the devices they have within their enterprise. IoT Gateways should be capable of connecting with multiple types of devices (including legacy) within the enterprise setting, and secondly they need to be robust enough such that enterprises can deploy these IoT Gateways in tough and rough environments, such as at locations with high temperatures or dust.

Some IoT use cases need Gateways to connect to the devices continuously apart from being able to make time-sensitive and real-time decisions based on data received from these devices. In such case, introducing latency is not an option, which typically is caused when data moves back and forth to the cloud. This means that IoT Gateways should be capable of performing analytics and real-time decisions.

And finally, the most important thing is security. Many industries, such as healthcare, pharma, banking, and financial services, are regulated, and for all such enterprises, it is essential that data is kept on-site, and hence IoT Gateways should have the capability to store data.

There are loads of IoT Gateways that are in the market, and choosing the right Gateway based on the enterprise-specific needs is extremely important to be successful in an IoT journey. An IoT Gateway has a major impact on the successful deployment of an IoT solution. A significant percentage of IoT projects face implementation and scalability issues due to the incorrect choice of Gateway. There is a need to carefully evaluate the right Gateway based on the IoT use cases enterprises desire to implement.

Choosing the Right Smart IoT Gateway

Choosing the right Gateway depends on several factors and is based on the use cases enterprises choose to implement. The seven key considerations are depicted in Figure 6-2.

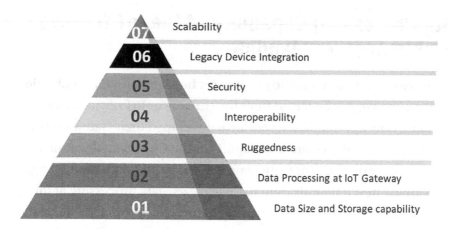

Figure 6-2. *Seven considerations for choosing a Smart IoT Gateway*

Data Size and Storage Capability

Many industrial IoT use cases require the deployment of hundreds of sensors, and in some cases there may be over ten thousand sensors at one location, and each sensor takes and transmits hundreds of readings per second. Analyzing the data volumes is an important step in the Gateway selection process. Secondly, many Gateway vendors have a limit to the number of devices that can be loaded on an IoT Gateway, and installing multiple IoT Gateways to achieve the scale may not be the wisest solution.

Industrial Gateways deployed in factories usually collect multiple sensor readings every second. However, situations such as network failures may arise, and as a result the Gateway will need to store this data locally while the network issues are being remedied.

Most Gateway models currently available on the market have storage capabilities, but a Gateway installed in the typical industrial setting needs to be able to store a significant amount of data and for longer periods of time. It is advisable therefore to choose a Gateway that allows for expansion of storage.

Data Processing Capability at the IoT Gateway Level Is Another Mandate

We discussed that traditional IoT Gateways had very limited capabilities to process data that is collected from the sensors or IoT devices. Many traditional Gateway manufacturers have developed their Gateways with zero processing or data storage capability at the Gateway, which means that all data need to be sent to the data centers or cloud for processing. Now with the new demands from IoT use cases, data processing at the edge is a mandate, and hence Smart IoT Gateways become the norm.

In most IoT solutions, not all the data from the sensors is required to be sent to the cloud for processing. It is required that a Gateway performs some preprocessing operations on the data obtained from the sensors before it sends the data to the cloud either for large-scale analytical processing or for data storage.

Based on the enterprise need, appropriate Gateways need to be selected.

Ruggedness of the IoT Gateway

Some enterprises need Gateways to be installed in an HVAC (Heating, Ventilation, and Air Conditioning) unit or at high altitudes, and, as a result, the Gateways would need to be robust and able to operate in extreme conditions.

Some Gateway models are designed to operate in harsh conditions of temperature ranges of –30° C to 70° C, altitude ranges of 15 m to 5000 m, and allow for high shock and vibration situations. Enterprises need to ensure that they select a Gateway that is suitable for their operating environment.

Interoperability (Connectivity Requirement)

Many IoT platforms utilize close-range connectivity options, such as Bluetooth and Ethernet, while Wi-Fi and Wireless LAN are used for longer-range connectivity needs. With the surge of IoT in industrial settings, almost all enterprises are choosing to monitor operations in their factories or plants remotely using their smartphones. There are Smart IoT Gateway models which do accommodate wider-range connectivity options to connect to mobile devices. However, not all IoT Gateways are created equal in this respect, and, generally, the less expensive the Gateway, the fewer connectivity options are provided, which is an important factor to consider.

As a general rule, standard protocols such as TCP/IP and HTTP should be supported by the Gateways in addition to the protocols which are used by devices within the enterprise. More specifically in an Industrial IoT context, apart from protocol connectivity, the Gateways must be able to integrate and interoperate with systems such as

- Enterprise asset management (EAM)

- Computerized maintenance management systems (CMMSs)

- Fleet management

- Condition-based maintenance (CBM)

- Manufacturing execution systems (MES)

- Maintenance, repair, and operations (MRO)

- Product life cycle management (PLM)

- Application portfolio management (APM)

- Field service management (FSM)

- Building management systems (BMSs)

Security

Securing Gateways is critical for the entire IoT platform. While most modern Gateways have built-in security options, it is still required to check the encryption standards the Gateway is using, whether the Gateway provides strong authentication processes as well as whether the Gateway can detect tampering. In addition, enterprises which choose to perform Device Management at the IoT Gateway level need to understand the security solutions the product offers from a Device Management perspective. Functionalities such as over-the-air software upgrades (SOTA) or secure DTLS data encryption are must-have features in Device Management.

An over-the-air (SOTA) update is the secured wireless delivery of new software, firmware, or other data to devices. Datagram Transport Layer Security (DTLS) enables enterprises to encrypt data packets that are sent between devices and Smart IoT Gateways.

Legacy Device Integration

Many enterprises have legacy devices that cannot be replaced, and these are true especially in an industrial setting such as manufacturing and in the healthcare industry.

Legacy devices operate on legacy connectivity, and the right Gateway needs to be chosen that can communicate with legacy devices.

Factories use legacy equipment and machinery with long life spans. It is often not economically viable or possible to upgrade or replace these devices in order to connect to the Internet directly. In these cases, the Gateway should be able to connect with this legacy equipment in order to ensure that all the data from the factory is integrated.

Scalability

Scalability will be key to handling the explosive growth in the Internet of Things (IoT). Smart IoT Gateways must have the ability to support an increasing number of connected devices, users, application features, and analytics capabilities, without any degradation in the quality of service.

IoT Gateway Comparisons

There are several companies existing in the market today that specialize in Smart IoT Gateways. In the context of this book, we will be discussing about commercial and Industrial IoT vendors.

Commercial IoT targets our daily environment outside of the home (consumer IoT). There is a set of applications that can be deployed in places we frequently visit, such as commercial office buildings, supermarkets, stores, hotels, healthcare facilities, or entertainment venues.

Industrial IoT Gateways are rugged by design and intended for critical systems and industrial environments.

Almost all industrial and commercial IoT solutions require Smart IoT Gateways because many IoT devices like sensors and actuators cannot connect to IT infrastructure. Device constraints such as small physical size, legacy protocols, extreme environmental conditions, remote locations, battery power, fast response time, and low cost require fit-for-purpose Smart IoT Gateways to perform protocol translations and enable data communication between devices. Another important function which Smart IoT Gateways perform is local analytics at the Gateway level, thereby shortening response times, improving reliability, and reducing upstream bandwidth. Another most crucial function required in Smart IoT Gateways is security. Very few IoT devices have enterprise-grade security, and especially legacy devices were never built keeping cyber security in view. Smart IoT Gateways should enable firewall protection that can insulate these vulnerable devices from enterprise assets and also from threats on the open Internet.

While the IoT market is still evolving, Dell and HPE have the most powerful commercial Smart IoT Gateways and are currently considered the market leaders. These Gateways are most relevant for enterprises that are looking for a lot of computation and bandwidth, such as implementing video surveillance. Dell has recently launched a bundle package around video surveillance. In general, any Gateway that can handle a video's density of data points can also handle factory automation, as well as predictive analytics. Some versions of Dell and HP IoT Gateways accommodate AI and machine learning as well.

Hewlett Packard Enterprise

Recognizing the commoditization of the IoT Gateway market at the low end, HPE has reserved its Edgeline brand for its self-sufficient Converged Edge Systems. These Gateways aggregate sensor data, convert it, and send it to the cloud for further processing. These Gateways also perform automated decision-making, storage, and control at the Gateway level. HPE's EL1000 and EL4000 Converged Edge Systems are examples of Gateways offered by HPE.

Dell

Dell offers the Edge Gateway 5000 Series, a ruggedized Gateway with a dual-core Atom processor for local analytics. An Atom processor is an ultra-low-voltage microprocessor by Intel Corporation designed to reduce electric consumption and power dissipation in comparison with ordinary processors of the Intel Core series.

Edge Gateway 5000 Series are engineered for industrial ranges of temperature, dust, and humidity. They are offered with operating systems such as Linux 0, Ubuntu Snappy, or Windows 10.

Though Dell and HP lead the IoT Gateway space, there are other mid-range IoT Gateway vendors who specialize in specific industries and use cases, some examples of which are mentioned in the following.

AAEON

AAEON offers four IoT Gateways for outdoor applications supporting low-power LoRa wireless networking as well as 4G and LTE cellular.

With wide operating temperatures, waterproof connectors, and resistance to dust, AAEON Gateways are aimed at energy metering, transportation, and other outdoor applications.

Digi International

Digi International is an American Industrial Internet of Things technology company headquartered in Hopkins, Minnesota.

Gateways such as SmartSense from Digi International are developed for specific verticals, such as food service and hospitality, facilities management, education, healthcare, transportation and logistics, and retail. For these verticals, SmartSense Gateways work well with protocols such as Wi-Fi and Bluetooth Low Energy.

Huawei

Huawei has specialized Gateways that cater to the video surveillance and smart city applications, such as streetlights and metering.

Summary

In this chapter, we started by discussing about the challenges which enterprises face while embarking on the IoT journey and how these can be mitigated – these are challenges such as security, data volumes, diverse products and platforms, challenges with IT and OT integration, and lack of standardized communication protocols and methodology to derive ROI for IoT projects.

We then discussed the seven factors that play a major role in selecting the right Smart IoT Gateway for IoT use cases, which are listed as follows:

1. Data size and storage

2. Data processing capability of the IoT Gateway

3. Ruggedness of the IoT Gateway

4. Interoperability

5. Security

6. Gateway integration capabilities with legacy devices

7. Scalability

We then discussed that Smart IoT Gateways should be capable of supporting the magnitude of OT devices so that enterprises can retrieve data from all devices that are part of the enterprise OT ecosystem. Apart from the scale, while most modern Gateways have built-in security options, it is still required to check the encryption standards the Gateway uses – whether the Gateway provides strong authentication processes as well as whether the Gateway can detect tampering. Very few IoT devices have enterprise-grade security, and since legacy devices were never built keeping cyber security in view, Smart IoT Gateways should have firewall protection that can insulate these vulnerable devices from enterprise assets and also from threats on the open Internet.

In the next chapter, we will discuss about the IoT Cloud Platform, which is the heart of the IoT Standards Reference Model.

CHAPTER 7

IoT Cloud Platform

A platform is a combination of software and hardware which includes an operating environment, storage, computing power, security, development tools, and many other common functions. Platforms abstract a lot of common functions away from the specific application logic. For example, regardless of whether you are trying to write an application to optimize fuel consumption or a classroom space, a lot of the underlying technology needs are essentially the same. Enterprises just need to focus on the specific problem they are solving and use common capabilities for computing power or storage or security. A good platform dramatically reduces the cost of developing and maintaining applications. Like an operating system for a laptop, a platform does a lot of things in the background that makes life easier and less expensive for developers, managers, and users.

A platform built for creating IoT solutions is called an IoT Platform. IoT platforms enable enterprises to build IoT solutions faster, cheaper, and better. There are IoT platforms of every shape and size. There are platforms for specific industries like commercial real estate and family health. Some focus on one type of devices; for example, there are at least a few platforms that focus on creating IoT solutions for augmented reality headsets, and some focus on a particular function, like manufacturing. There is a need for disparate IoT devices to connect seurely, efficiently and interoperate with each other. IoT platforms addresses this need and therfore have become a backbone of IoT deployments. Though on one side the importance of IoT Platforms has increased significantly, there are a

V. Upadrista, *IoT Standards with Blockchain*,
https://doi.org/10.1007/978-1-4842-7271-8_7

huge number of IoT platforms that are emerging in the market. By the end of 2019, there were around 620 publicly known IoT platforms, which was more than twice as many as in 2015. With such an increase in the number of IoT platforms, it becomes essential for enterprises to select the right platform that can support them in their industry-specific use cases and at the same time will be able to suffice their next ten years of IoT demands. At the end, enterprises will not want to replace IoT platforms every few years and need a solution that can last longer.

The essential capabilities required in an IoT Platform range from connectivity and network management, IoT Device Management, data acquisition, processing analysis and visualization, application development (creating and managing IoT applications), storage, and security.

With the introduction of Smart IoT Gateways in the IoT Standards Reference Model, some of the functions are handled by the IoT Gateways. As an example, in most IoT scenarios, connectivity and network management is performed by an IoT Gateway apart from data collection, processing, and some part of analysis. However, this differs on a case-by-case basis, and a careful assessment needs to be performed to decide the most optimal and efficient model that can determine which tasks need to be performed by the Smart IoT Gateway and which ones by the IoT Platform. Based on this assessment, an appropriate IoT platform needs to be chosen.

IoT Basic Six

Performance is one of the key considerations for choosing an IoT Platform, but there are other important factors to be considered. There is no easy answer to which IoT cloud platform to choose; however, before even going into the details of how efficient a specific platform is developed to support IoT solutions, it is essential to shortlist IoT cloud Platform providers based on the six general characteristics as depicted in Figure 7-1, which are called the IoT Basic Six.

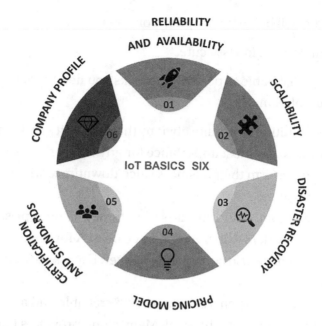

Figure 7-1. Six general characteristics while choosing a cloud platform

Reliability and Availability

A reliable and highly available IT platform is the basic need for any enterprise to do business. Reliability is the probability of a system or a component (hosted in the cloud) for performing the required functions in a period of time without failure. Availability is the time the platform provider guarantees that data and services are available in a given period of time.

As an example, when you access an application or service hosted in the cloud or data center, the following are the basic expectations from a reliability standpoint:

- The app or service is up and running.

- You can access what you need from any device at any time from any location.

123

- There will be no interruptions or downtime.

- Your connection is secure.

- You will be able to perform the tasks you need to get your job done.

From the definition, it is quite obvious that reliability and availability of a cloud platform is of utmost importance for any enterprise that wants to use the cloud to perform their business since downtimes will have a direct impact on the business.

Shortlisting a cloud platform starts from here, and enterprises need to clearly look for providers who not only agree on SLA for high availability and reliability but have also consistently delivered to these SLAs in the last several years.

In a perfect world, systems should be 100% reliable and available, but that is probably not an attainable goal. Many cloud providers have an SLA of 99.99% reliability target. Availability is typically documented as a percent of time per year, for example, 99.999% uptime means enterprises will be unable to access resources for no more than about five minutes per year.

Scalability

The second most important element that influences the choice of a cloud provider is scalability. Cloud scalability refers to how well systems can react and adapt to changing demands. As enterprises grow, they want to be able to seamlessly add resources without losing quality of service or interruptions. As the demand for resources decreases, enterprises want to be able to quickly and efficiently downscale systems so that they need not have to pay for resources they do not need. A resource means an operating system, an application, a specific hardware, tools, or devices.

However, there is more to scalability in the cloud than simply adding or removing resources as needed, some of which are mentioned in the following.

Cloud Elasticity

Cloud elasticity is the term used to refer to how well cloud services are able to add and remove resources on demand. Elasticity is important because enterprises want to ensure that their clients and employees have access to the right number of resources they needed and they are paying for what they are using. Cloud elasticity should be automatic and seamless. People accessing cloud services should not be able to notice that resources are added or dropped. They should just have the confidence that they can access and use resources without interruptions.

Vertical Scaling

Vertical scaling (or "scaling up") refers to upgrading a single resource. For example, installing more memory or storage capacity to an existing server. In a physical, on-premises setup, enterprises would need to shut down the server to install the updates, but in the cloud world, this can be accomplished without bringing the servers down.

Horizontal Scaling

This term is used to describe "building out" a system with additional components. For example, enterprises can add processing power or more memory to a server by linking it with other servers. Horizontal scaling is a necessary capability to validate while choosing a cloud provider. Enterprises should be able to add additional hardware or software resources with minimal impact to provide redundancy and ensure that services remain reliable and available.

125

Autoscaling

Autoscaling is an important cloud computing feature that lets enterprises automatically manage the different types of scalability in the cloud. Cloud providers, such as Amazon Web Services, Microsoft Azure, and Google Cloud, offer autoscaling to enable consistent performance regardless of the current demand on resources, and it is another key element to be validated while choosing a cloud platform.

Disaster Recovery

The third basic feature that determines the platform choice is the ability of the cloud provider to react during a disaster. Disaster recovery (DR) is an area of security planning that aims to protect an organization from the effects of significant negative and unexpected events such as floods, fire, and other natural calamities. Having a disaster recovery in place enables an organization to maintain or quickly resume mission-critical functions following a disruption. Disaster recovery in cloud computing means storing critical data and applications in cloud storage and failing over to a secondary site in case of a disaster. Disaster recovery is a very key feature which needs to be factored while choosing a cloud provider. Enterprises need to understand the provider disaster recovery provisions, processes, and their ability to support data preservation expectations (including recovery time objectives).

Data at rest generally refers to data stored in persistent storage (disk, tape), while data in use generally refers to data being processed by a computer central processing unit (CPU) or in random access memory (RAM, also referred to as main memory or simply memory).

Data in transit, also referred to as data in motion and data in flight, is defined into two categories: information that flows over the public or untrusted network such as the Internet and data that flows in the confines of a private network such as a corporate or enterprise local area network.

Data Security

Data security forms the fourth key consideration and is the most important element while choosing an IoT Platform. Cloud data protection is the practice of securing enterprise data in a cloud environment, wherever that data is located, whether it is at rest or in motion, and whether it is managed internally by the company or externally by a third party. Enterprises need to make sure that the provider they choose meets the strict security standards based on their regional and industry needs. Enterprises need to verify if cloud providers are compliant with basic standards like the ISO 27000 series and if their certifications are valid. Enterprises also need to look at platform providers' compliance with data protection and privacy laws and regulations, such as the General Data Protection Regulation, or GDPR, in the EU; the Health Insurance Portability and Accountability Act of 1996, or HIPAA, in the United States; and others.

Server location where enterprise data and application will reside is also important to understand as different local laws may apply, and enterprises need to be 100% sure of having control regarding the jurisdiction in which their data is stored, processed, and managed.

Apart from data security, cloud security is also an essential element to understand during a platform selection. Cloud security consists of a set of policies, controls, procedures, and technologies that work together to protect cloud-based systems, data, and infrastructure. From authenticating access to filtering traffic, platform providers need to have cloud security that can be configured to the exact needs of the business.

Platform as a service (PaaS) is a type of cloud computing offering in which a service provider delivers a platform to clients, enabling them to develop, run, and manage business applications without the need to build and maintain the infrastructure such software development processes typically require.

Infrastructure as a service (IaaS) is a form of cloud computing that provides virtualized computing resources over the Internet. IaaS is one of the three main categories of cloud computing services, alongside software as a service (SaaS) and platform as a service (PaaS).

Software as a service[1] is a software licensing and delivery model in which software is licensed on a subscription basis and is centrally hosted. It is sometimes referred to as "on-demand software" and was formerly referred to as "software plus services" by Microsoft.[2]

It is very essential for enterprises to validate the enterprise requirements vis-à-vis the platform capabilities in the area of security, such as authentication, encryption, and monitoring capabilities platform providers have.

Pricing Model

One of the benefits of the cloud is that enterprises pay for the services and resources they use. Rather than being presented with a flat fee, cloud providers operate on a pay-as-you-use pricing model. Each cloud

---

[1] Panker, Jon; Lewis, Mark; Fahey, Evan; Vasquez, Melvin Jafet (August 2007)." How do you pronounce IT?". TechTarget. Retrieved 24 May 2012

[2] "Microsoft describes software plus services." InfoWorld. 26 July 2007. Retrieved 7 February 2017

service provider has a unique bundle of services and pricing models. Different providers have unique price advantages for different products. Typically, pricing variables are based on the period of usage with some providers allowing for by-the-minute usage as well as discounts for longer commitments.

The most common model for SaaS-based products is on a per-user, per-month basis, though there may be different levels based on storage requirements, contractual commitments, or access to advanced features.

PaaS and IaaS pricing models are more granular, with costs for specific resources or "resource sets" consumption. Aside from financial competitiveness, enterprises need to look for flexibility in terms of resource variables but also in terms of speed to provision and deprovision. An application architecture that allows enterprises to scale different elements independently means one can use cloud resources more efficiently.

Certifications and Standards

Providers that comply with recognized standards and quality frameworks demonstrate an adherence to industry best practices and standards. While standards may not determine which platform to choose, they can be very helpful in shortlisting potential IoT Platform providers. For instance, if security is a priority, enterprises need to look at IoT Platforms accredited with certifications like ISO 27001 or the government's Cyber Essentials Scheme or COBIT.

Company Profile

It is always advisable to work with a company that is reputable and has a strong record of stability and has no history of legal issues or data breach. The choice of the platform provider should depend on the healthy financial position of the company. There are more than 500 cloud providers in the market that promise IoT cloud solutions, and hence measuring the service providers based on their profile becomes extremely important.

Specific Capabilities

So far, we discussed about the basic six capabilities that help enterprises in prescreening the cloud platform providers. In my experience with these basic six features, enterprises can filter their IoT Platform providers to less than ten. Though this is the good first milestone achieved, it is quite essential to understand that the most important step for any enterprise to succeed in IoT is to choose a platform based on the provider specialization and capabilities in IoT. An IoT Platform should have enough breadth and depth of capabilities specific to IoT solutions, based on the enterprise business and use cases. If this step goes wrong, enterprises risk themselves toward failed IoT projects.

Today, there is no one-size-fits-all platform for an IoT solution. Choosing a platform should start with a good understanding of the enterprise IoT strategy. It is essential to identify the kinds of problems an enterprise is trying to solve using IoT, get a short list of likely solutions and use cases, and try to determine where you will need specialization and depth. If enterprises have an idea of what kind of business problem they are solving and where the biggest challenges are, you will be able to quickly come to a short list of platforms.

The good news is that, with the introduction of the IoT Gateway in the IoT Standards Reference Model, some of the core features are handled at this level, and a reminder of the capabilities is required in an IoT Platform. This makes a lot of sense since such an architecture brings in autonomy within the architecture. Based on the specific needs, enterprises can choose which capabilities are required at the IoT Gateway level and which ones are required at an IoT Platform level.

The four core capabilities that guide enterprises in choosing an IoT platform are depicted in Figure 7-2 and listed as follows:

1. Connectivity

2. Device Management

3. Application enablement platform

4. Scalability (device level, data storage, and analytics)

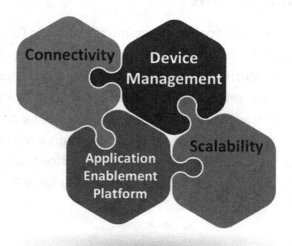

Figure 7-2. *Four core capabilities while choosing a cloud platform*

Connectivity

The first one is the connectivity. In most of the use cases, the Smart IoT Gateway manages the communication with the IoT devices. The IoT Platform should be capable of communicating with the Smart IoT Gateway in a seamless manner and sending and receiving data both in real time and in batch.

Batch data processing is a model of processing high volumes of data where a group of transactions is collected over a period of time and transferred to an IoT Platform in a batch. In contrast, real-time data processing involves a continual input, process, and output of data from Smart IoT Gateways to the IoT Platform. Data must be processed in a small time period (or near real time).

Device Management

Device Management is a very important function in an IoT Standards Reference Model and refers to the processes of provisioning and authenticating, configuring, maintaining, monitoring, and diagnosing connected devices operating as part of an IoT ecosystem. Some enterprises choose the IoT Gateway to perform Device Management, and some prefer to do it at an IoT Platform level. Appropriate decisions need to be made based on enterprise business and the use cases. Device Management broadly has three different functions as depicted in Figure 7-3.

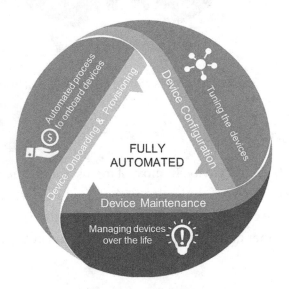

Figure 7-3. *Device Management functions*

Device Onboarding and Provisioning

Many enterprises follow a manual process where devices are activated in the field, configured on the network using IT, and registered with a device owner in an IoT platform. This is a time-intensive process and at the same time can lead to security breaches as demonstrated by recent large-scale attacks where device manufacturers have shipped default credentials that were compromised by hackers using botnet-style attacks. A botnet is a collection of Internet-connected devices infected by malware that allow hackers to control them. Cybercriminals use botnets to instigate botnet attacks, which include malicious activities such as credential leaks, unauthorized access, data theft, and DoS attacks.

A denial-of-service (DoS) attack is a cyber-attack in which the perpetrator seeks to make a machine or network resource unavailable to its intended users by temporarily or indefinitely disrupting services.

Some enterprises have claimed that manually adding one device can take over 30 minutes per device. Imagine a factory installing 10,000 smart light bulbs, all of which needs to be onboarded on an IoT platform. Effectively, this means that in a manual way an enterprise will need to spend 300,000 person hours to complete the installation. The key demand of many enterprises today is to reduce the onboard time for IoT devices on the platform. In an Industrial IoT case study, an enterprise has tens of thousands of devices to onboard, and in such a large setting, manual processes lead to significant costs and efforts. While choosing an IoT Platform, enterprises need to look for IoT platforms which can bring down installation time and get IoT devices online faster and in a secured and automated way. There are IoT platforms available in the market which have created a zero-touch approach, making it possible for IoT devices to dynamically discover the IoT platform at power-on for automatic registration. Not all enterprises will need such features, and careful analytics needs to be performed based on which IoT platform needs to be chosen.

When adding an IoT device, enterprises need to ensure that only trusted devices are added to the enterprise IoT ecosystem. Device authentication is therefore very essential and is the act of securely establishing the identity of the device and ensuring that it can be trusted. With device authentication, enterprises can be assured that the device is genuine and is running trusted software and is working on behalf of a trusted user.

Enterprises need to ensure that they choose a platform that can support automatic and secure device onboarding. As an example, once a new device on the field is powered on, the IoT Platform should be able to locate the device and automatically onboard the device on the IoT platform in a completely secured way using methods such as public key encryption. Public key encryption, also known as asymmetric encryption, uses two separate keys instead of one shared one: a public key and a private key. Public key encryption is an important technology for Internet security.

Device Configuration

As soon as a device gets onboarded, device configuration comes into play. Device configuration is the process of fine-tuning the onboarded devices beyond their default settings, such as changing password or upgrading with latest firmware. A flexible and intuitive configuration mechanism should be available with the IoT platform that can enable enterprises to design the behavior of their smart fleet not only in times when devices perform as planned but also to react on the fly in case of any failures that come along the way. A summation of all the IoT device part of an enterprise IoT ecosystem is referred to as smart fleet.

Device Maintenance

Device maintenance deals with the process of improving device performance or eliminating technical issues in the devices. This includes installing software fixes or patches remotely or pushing upgrades to all devices in the fleet of all IoT devices at the same time without manual intervention.

Device maintenance also deals with recommending or performing repair actions when a device is down. When equipment goes down, failure data from various sources can be gathered, aggregated, and analyzed in real time, and repair actions can be initiated automatically by the IoT Platform, or actions can be recommended to the technician if necessary. Enterprises need to validate the exhaustiveness of the solutions offered by IoT Platform providers in this respect.

Asset-intensive industries face a range of challenges when it comes to ensuring mission-critical plants and equipment operate at maximum efficiency and uptime, and customer service commitments are met, as even the smallest disruption to service can lead to costly penalties or, worse, churn. Enterprises need to understand how their products and assets are performing so that they can optimize their use and better anticipate issues and failures. This is the main reason why remote monitoring and maintenance has an important role to play in an IoT ecosystem. Monitoring and diagnosing includes not only giving enterprises the ability to better monitor the proper functioning of their products and plant machinery but also enabling them to prevent costly breakdown and fixes and improve customer service.

Application Enablement Platforms (IoT Platform with Superior Application Development Capabilities)

A very important feature required in an IoT Platform is the ability to support developers in creating IoT applications with ease. Enterprises need to select an IoT platform that has superior application development capabilities which can offer the full range of tools needed to get an IoT application up and running in the shortest time possible. The platform should have solutions enabling developers to rapidly create, test, and deploy an IoT application or service. The platform should have prewritten applications that developers can use to speed up their development. These platforms typically should include software and devices, along with development and deployment solutions that make it easier to get an IoT application up and running. The benefit is that such platforms take care of the development, network configuration, and installation typically done by developers, which potentially saves a lot of time and development efforts.

Choosing an IoT Platform with superior application development capabilities simplifies a lot of the complexity in the IoT use case realization by reducing the time needed to create an IoT solution or a product with lower cost of ownership.

Another important aspect to validate when choosing an IoT platform is the capability of the platform to connect and integrate with other enterprise applications such as the ERP (enterprise resource planning) or MES (manufacturing execution systems) application. Manufacturing execution systems are computerized systems used in manufacturing to track and document the transformation of raw materials to finished goods. ERP is a system that automates business functions like production, sales quoting, and accounting.

Application development capabilities in an IoT Platform impact the value realization. An IoT platform needs to be carefully chosen, keeping in mind the developer's ease of using the platform to perform development. Apart from the ease of development and capability to integrate with other applications, scalability is very essential. As an example, the platform should be able to support developers in creating fixed applications, such as web-based applications as well as mobile or desktop applications.

Choosing a platform with superior development capabilities reduces the time to market and risk of development. There are several matured IoT Platform vendors that provide valuable services that simplify the development of IoT applications. They have prebuilt models for popular devices like motion sensors and at the same time provide a platform for designing a custom module for a unique use case. Using these platforms, developers can easily connect different IoT devices and services, determine their interactions, and build IoT applications faster compared to traditional custom coding.

So in summary, the three main application considerations when choosing a platform are

1. What applications are available out of the box?

2. What is the application development environment like?

3. What are the common enterprise application interfaces?

Many platforms will include one or more applications that may be of value out of the box, like the stock market or weather apps that ship with iPhones. Sometimes, very simple applications are the most popular and effective. One manager in a store told us, "I'd be delighted to have an app that just tells me which units in my shop are switched on or off."

Scalability

Scalability is another important feature which every enterprise needs to thoroughly validate while choosing an IoT Platform. In an IoT platform context, scalability comes majorly from three different perspectives.

The first one is the ability of the IoT platform to onboard a magnitude of devices with different connectivity protocols, second is the ability of the IoT Platform to store massive amount of data, and third is the capability to perform massive analytics processes. All these three elements form the core to succeed in an IoT project.

(Large-Scale) Device Onboarding Capabilities

If an enterprise decides to perform device onboarding by an IoT Platform, it is essential that they choose a platform that is capable of onboarding as many devices as required, and the upper limit can be decided by the enterprise business and the industry they operate. As an example, Tesla had thousands of IoT devices in 2004, but today it has more than one million devices in their units, and any company as big as Tesla will have similar number of devices. An IoT platform chosen for such industries should have the ability to scale and connect to millions of devices at once. In another example, a smart building may need thousands of small IoT devices such as smart bulbs to be onboarded on the IoT platform, whereas in a factory setting, many require a few hundreds of large IoT devices for their use cases.

Many commercial-grade IoT Platforms today have the flexibility to onboard as many devices as necessary on their platform.

Apart from the capability of onboarding multiple IoT devices on the platform, the ease of performing Device Management is a critical factor to be validated while choosing an IoT Platform.

Data Storage and IoT Analytics

From a scalability perspective, another most important and mandatory capability that is expected from an IoT Platform is the scalability of data storage. Scalability is key to handling the explosive growth in data since IoT is all about data generated by devices which is huge. IoT platforms must have superior data storage and analytic capabilities. The objective of IoT analytics is to gain value from large volumes of data generated by devices connected via the Internet of Things (IoT).

With the cloud, data storage is available on demand, and hence enterprises need to be least bothered about data storage. Almost all IoT Platform providers use the cloud for data storage, and therefore by default there will be enough storage to collect and process massive IoT data streams.

A **data lake** is a centralized repository that allows you to store all your structured and unstructured data at any scale.

Data swamp is data which is of limited use.

However, in an IoT ecosystem, storage is not a challenge, but the ability of IoT Platforms to have solutions that can store the right data in the right way is essential. In an IoT architecture, there are thousands of sensors collecting huge volumes of both structured and unstructured data, such as temperature reading as well as video and audio footage. Almost all IoT Platforms use data lakes to store this raw data. The benefits of data lakes are that they can grow indefinitely, integrate with many processing and analytics tools, and provide a relatively low cost of storage. However, to enable analytics on IoT data, organizations need to plan their storage carefully. Just dumping data into a data lake with no prior treatment can create a data swamp. Enterprises need to ensure that they save only the required data to a data lake, and secondly data should be stored in a format that enables analysis without the need to perform heavy corrections on the data. The IoT Platform should be able to support such a need.

Though we speak about data storage at the IoT Platform level, it is not always necessary that enterprises should transfer all data (processing work) to the cloud. In many scenarios, a combination of the IoT Platform in the cloud and the Smart IoT Gateway is put to action to strike the right balance between scale, cost, latency, and data privacy. There may be some data storage and analytics processes that need to happen at Smart Gateways and the rest in the cloud or vice versa. With that in mind, enterprises need to make sure that they have connected systems that can support such hybrid workflows to enable seamless migration from the edge (Smart IoT Gateway) to the cloud (IoT Cloud Platform).

Irrespective of where data storage and analytics happen (i.e., at an IoT Gateway level or IoT Platform level), an IoT platform needs a robust data processing engine (pipeline) that can perform data curation (cleaning, enrichment, transformation) functions on streaming data. The data pipeline needs to be well balanced in its ability to sustain a continuous flow of streaming data. It must also be able to handle situations such as a temporary surge in the data, performance issues, and disruptions in downstream systems.

Proof of Concept (POC)

After shortlisting a platform vendor, it is essential that enterprises run a few proofs of concepts (POCs) to test the platform performance and capabilities using different technical criteria, such as the amount and quality of functionalities, tools and services, usability, security, and interoperability. The cost of the platform should also be validated in this step.

Instead of asking platform vendors to present some hypothetical capabilities, enterprises should implement POCs after setting up a real-world testbed which resembles their actual product or production process and contains actual data sets from their products or factories.

In essence, enterprises need to create POCs to explore and "play" with the platforms to see how they work and what advantages they can get from them based on real usage scenarios.

Summary

This chapter primarily discussed about choosing the right IoT Cloud Platform for enterprises to be successful in their IoT journey. Though there is no easy answer to which IoT cloud platform to choose, this chapter provided a guidance toward the same based on the six general characteristics and four core capabilities:

- The six general characteristics to be validated while shortlisting an IoT Cloud Platform include reliability, availability, and scalability plus the ability of the cloud provider to support disaster recovery. Security is another important element to be validated. The pricing model and the certification and standards possessed by the platform are the other two areas to be validated.

- The four core capabilities that guide enterprises in choosing an IoT platform are connectivity, Device Management, application enablement platform, and scalability (device level, data storage, and analytics).

Based on the preceding guidance, enterprises can choose the right IoT Cloud Platform.

In the next chapter, we will discuss about the importance of security and its applicability at each layer in an IoT Standards Reference Model.

CHAPTER 8

Security in IoT

OT systems in an enterprise are the cash registers – whether it is a power generation unit, car manufacturing unit, oil refining, or chemical development, OT systems generate money for enterprises. All focus has therefore traditionally been placed on making sure that the OT systems that produce the end products have been designed in a way that they are very safe, highly efficient, and productive with "long-lived missions." A long-lived mission means that an OT system of critical infrastructure is expected to run 24/7 and 365 days a year for several decades. Due to such a need, major patching or upgrading cycles do not happen for years, and therefore the types of vulnerabilities that exist live a very long time in those systems.

In the IT era, we have now come across several security incidents. Each and every time there is a new bug, the manufacturer pushes a patch to address it. It is a reactive approach, as with every new attack, enterprises respond with forensic investigations that ultimately lead to patching and ongoing monitoring to stop the problem from reappearing. However, such an approach is not possible in the OT world. A small incident can not only cause the plant to shut down leading to millions of dollars losses, but there is also the chance of human losses and accidents due to cyber-attacks. On the other hand, there are trade secrets such as recipes that are often loaded on the OT control systems that need to be protected. This is one

© Venkatesh Upadrista 2021
V. Upadrista, *IoT Standards with Blockchain*,
https://doi.org/10.1007/978-1-4842-7271-8_8

of the reasons why OT security is at the very top of security concerns in IoT. Unlike the IT world, OT systems have

- Not learned from cyber-attacks

- Not undergone upgrades like IT systems

- More aged infrastructure that have less controls since OT systems were never built to be exposed to the outside world

- Tools and systems that have not been developed to solve cyber-attacks

This is the biggest challenge which is existing in the OT world, and it is clear that after IT-OT integration, cyber-attackers will try to enter the OT system via the IT systems. This is the biggest challenge in the IoT industry today.

We have seen in the past a rushed approach for IT and OT integration. One example is the smart metering payday of 2008–2011. This was the time when there was a lot of investment in the industry for new kinds of technology on the operational side of the house. Wireless systems were making it possible to gather information to reduce operational costs, thereby achieving operational efficiency. During this time, security in OT systems took a backseat, and after some time the industry saw cyber-attacks on smart meters. As an example, some smart meter settings were changed by individuals so that meter readings did not go up, by placing large-sized magnets on the meters. This was the evolution of IoT where cyber security was thought of as a secondary requirement, and because of this some utility providers lost millions of dollars.

You can either think about cyber security at the start while embarking in an IoT journey or you can do it later. The effect of doing it later could unfortunately lead to dire situations such as shutting down the business entirely, as there are undoubtedly a number of unforeseen consequences that could ultimately lead to disasters.

The current level of security awareness in the industry toward IoT is still quite diverse. From my experience speaking to several enterprises in the OT world, nearly 40% of enterprises believe that being isolated from external threats is a solution to being secure, and therefore they tend to be disconnected from the outside world. These enterprises consider isolation as a strategy to protect themselves against cyber risks and therefore have never been able to take advantage of the technology existing in the market. These are the ones who are at risk of losing business since there are better and cheaper ways to conduct it, which their competitors have likely already adopted.

On the other end of the spectrum, there are fewer enterprises, say 10% of them, that are aware and are diligent on the advancements in the IT industry and have increased their cyber security posture year after year to stay ahead of emerging threats. There are other organizations that are in the middle of both these categories; these are the ones that are in the regulated industries and have a compliance aspect in their mandate. They enhance their cyber security posture to simply meet their compliance requirements. Since these enterprises have not thought of cyber security beyond compliance, they are at a high risk of falling prey to cyber-attacks.

There are matured cyber security practices in the IT world, which are maturing in the OT world as well, with the popularity IoT has gained in the last few years. Due to this, cyber security practices in existence today for IoT are able to address many of the complex issues of protecting critical infrastructure and data in an IoT world.

IoT is the reality of the future. For enterprises to reach the next level of maturity, to achieve higher productivity and to deliver better and faster outcomes and be cheaper applying IoT to their business model is the only option. Many enterprises have already realized this fact; however, being connected in a world where OT has never been thought of from a cyber security perspective poses the highest degree of risk to enterprises. Often, I have come across two types of enterprises – the ones that are striving for this productivity outcome by compromising security, and others that do not want to move toward IoT. Neither of these are the right option. The only option is to address cyber security and take actions to secure both IT and OT, which is a mandate for every enterprise.

In most cyber-attack cases on OT systems, it is a trial and error process to hack the system. Hackers are just looking to see what they can access remotely and trying to find ways to get into an operational system. I have also seen the opposite – in some cases, there have been situations where attacks have been launched on the OT side, and these hacked systems were then used to gain access to the IT systems. This is what I call a pivotal attack, and these types of attacks are on the rise.

As we have discussed so far, security cannot be centered around IT and OT in silos in IoT. They need to be operating together to prevent cyber-attacks, which takes us into the next question: what does it mean to secure the IoT systems? There are three main components, as depicted in Figure 8-1, that are necessary in order to effectively secure critical infrastructure in an IoT ecosystem.

Figure 8-1. *Components to secure OT infrastructure*

Industrial mindset – The industrial mindset comes first in IoT. This means enterprises on an IoT journey need to take into account things such as the missions of the OT systems, which are often focused around zero downtime and safety as a practice. It is also concerned with the engineering discipline and the quality focus that typically goes into designing these industrial systems and recognizing that these systems are the cash registers of the business.

Cyber security – The second key aspect is to have cyber security expertise when enterprises deal with OT systems. Cyber security personnel need to understand the similarities and differences between IT and OT and should be experts in this particular field. The types of technologies that are used in some layers of OT or critical infrastructure are very similar to IT. There are workstations, standard software stacks, or standard applications, but as we reach deeper into the OT system, there are different kinds of technology stacks, embedded equipment such as real-time operating systems, and industrial proprietary protocols that are used to connect these systems together. Cyber security experts need to understand the differences in the technology and the differences in the vulnerabilities that OT systems have since these are legacy products with long-lived missions and bring in the right solutions to address these challenges. The consequences of a compromise can mean a danger to life.

Purpose-built technology – The third area that needs focus is purpose-built technology. This means that enterprises need to look at technologies that are built to provide deep visibility and protection specifically for industrial connected systems that will be part of IoT implementations. Cyber experts need to look at the specific nature of the risk at each layer of the OT system and make sure that the protective measure that will be employed inside that system is going to support each particular mission. They will need to deeply understand the protocols that are used to connect these systems together, speed of data, and information transferred and not introduce any unintended latency or jitter as such inefficiencies can bring the OT systems down. As an example, the patching cycles often tend to be more rapid on the IT side than they are on the OT side of the house. Many OT systems may take years or months to put a patch or protection in place simply because of the operational mission of the particular OT system. From a purpose-built technology perspective, the main difference we see here is that there is a whole host of standardized protocols on the IT side. In the OT side, there are a lot of pieces of equipment that have been built around proprietary technology and proprietary protocols which glue the OT systems together and connect them to allow machine-to-machine interaction. The protective measures that are employed in an IT world are often based on standardized protocols, whereas on the OT side, we will get into all kinds of esoteric and proprietary protocols that are the systems used to communicate with each other. It is essential for enterprises to utilize security technologies and platforms that are built purposefully for all such OT systems.

Secure by Design (Securing the Whole IoT Ecosystem)

Security by design is the inclusion of security design principles, technology, and governance at every stage of the IoT journey and within all layers of the IoT Standards Reference Model. When an organization looks at creating, deploying, and leveraging connected technology to drive business, security must be integrated into every component, tier, and application to preserve the integrity of the IoT solution and minimize the risk of cyber threats.

IoT systems are highly complex, requiring end-to-end security solutions that span cloud and connectivity layers, and should be able to support resource-constrained IoT devices that often are not powerful enough to support traditional security solutions. There is no single silver bullet, and security must be comprehensive at each layer within an IoT ecosystem, or attackers can simply exploit the weakest link. Though traditional Information Technology (IT) systems drive and handle data from IoT devices, IoT devices themselves will have unique additional security needs that need to be handled.

IoT security needs to be considered starting from device procurement (buy devices with security built in), device protection, API security, Smart IoT Gateway security, patch management, hardware security, and IoT Cloud Platform security.

These foundations can be combined to form powerful and easy-to-deploy security foundations in an IoT ecosystem to mitigate the vast majority of security threats to the Internet of Things, including advanced and sophisticated threats. However, enterprises need to understand that there is no single solution that can cover IoT security in full. Each use case and every industry (automotive, energy, manufacturing, healthcare, financial services, government, retail, logistics, aviation, consumer, and beyond) is unique, and a security solution needs to be decided based on the use case and the threats pertaining to a particular industry and use case.

Buy Devices with Built-in Security

Device manufacturers need to ensure that security is built into the devices, and enterprises procuring new devices should carefully select the ones that have built-in security. Another aspect while purchasing new devices is to understand that devices which have hardcoded credentials are not ideal candidates for an enterprise IoT ecosystem. Enterprises should be able to update the default credentials before the device is put into action. Devices need to be updated using a strong password or multifactor authentication or biometrics where possible.

Technologies such as elliptic curve cryptography have revolutionized the industry especially for security-related to resource-constrained devices, and enterprises need to ensure that such security-enabled devices become part of their IoT ecosystem. Symantec which is a leading Certificate Authority (CA) has already embedded such security features into more than a billion IoT devices, helping mutually authenticate a wide range of devices, including cellular base stations, televisions, and more.

Identity management for devices is quite essential in an IoT context. Each IoT device needs to have a unique identifier to understand what the device is, how it behaves, the other devices it interacts with, and the proper security measures that should be taken for that device.

Not all enterprises can deploy new IoT devices, and they need to coexist with existing devices and equipment, many of which are legacy. Many of such legacy devices and equipment still need to be connected to the IoT ecosystem. There is no single solution to secure such devices, and enterprises need to develop security solutions based on the devices and equipment that are being connected to the Internet.

Table 8-1 provides a generic view on the traditional IT and OT security solutions and how a combination of these two can secure enterprises after IT-OT integration. This is a partial list which provides a starting point for enterprises to manage their security posters in an IT-OT-integrated world. Each enterprise needs to tailor their own cyber security solutions based on the operational systems in use currently.

***Table 8-1.** Traditional IT and OT Security Solutions*

Service	Description	Traditional IT	Traditional OT	IT-OT Integration (IoT)
Firewall	Acts as a gatekeeper between a network and the wider Internet. Filters incoming and in some cases outgoing traffic by comparing data packets against predefined rules and policies.	✓		✓

(continued)

Table 8-1. (*continued*)

Service	Description	Traditional IT	Traditional OT	IT-OT Integration (IoT)
Intrusion prevention service and intrusion detection service	Deep packet inspection; protects against malware entry into the network.	✔		✔
Access controls	Controls which users have access to the network or to sensitive sections of the network.	✔		✔
Antivirus and antimalware software	A software used to prevent, detect, and remove malware.	✔		✔
Application security	Refers to the combination of hardware, software, and best practices used within an enterprise to monitor security issues and risks during application development and operations.	✔		✔
Behavioral analytics	A method by which abnormal behaviors are identified and resolved.	✔		✔

(*continued*)

Table 8-1. (*continued*)

Service	Description	Traditional IT	Traditional OT	IT-OT Integration (IoT)
Data loss prevention	A technology which prevents an employee from sharing valuable company information or sensitive data, unwittingly or with ill intent, outside the network.	✓		✓
Network monitoring and visibility	A technology to automatically generate views into all network communication, enabling policy creation and automated enforcement.		✓	✓
Network segmentation	A capability to manage data flow between IT networks and OT environments.		✓	✓

(*continued*)

Table 8-1. (*continued*)

Service	Description	Traditional IT	Traditional OT	IT-OT Integration (IoT)
ICS vulnerability intelligence	A platform that automatically detects industrial malware, including zero-day vulnerabilities. A zero-day vulnerability is a software security flaw that is known to the software vendor but does not have a patch in place to fix the flaw.		✓	✓
OT firewalls	A technology that offers policy-driven and centralized management capability and puts enterprises in control of their industrial environments.		✓	✓

Protecting Devices

Protecting devices against attacks requires both code signing and runtime protection.

Code signing is the process of digitally signing executables and scripts to confirm the software author and guarantee that the code has not been altered or corrupted since it was signed. Runtime Self-Protection (RSP) is a security solution designed to provide personalized protection to applications running on the devices. It takes advantage of the insight into an application's internal data and state to enable it to identify threats at runtime that may have otherwise been overlooked by other security solutions. Code signing cryptographically ensures code has not been tampered after being "signed" as safe for the device. All critical devices, whether a sensor or a hub, should be configured to only run signed code and never run unsigned code. Still, devices must be protected long after code begins running. Host-based protections help here. A host-based security is a piece of firewall software that runs on an individual computer or device connected to a network. These types of firewalls are a granular way to protect the individual hosts from viruses and malware and to control the spread of these harmful infections throughout the network.

Host-based protection provides hardening, lockdown, whitelisting, sandboxing, network-facing intrusion prevention, and many such security features for a variety of IoT devices.

API Security

The application program (or programming) interface, or API, ties devices and the complete IoT ecosystem together. IoT APIs are the points of interaction between an IoT device and the Internet and/or other elements and systems within the IoT network.

API security is concerned with the transfer of data through APIs that are connected to the Internet. It is essential for enterprises to protect the integrity of data being sent from IoT devices to Smart IoT Gateways to the IoT Cloud Platform or back-end systems and ensure only authorized devices and applications communicate with APIs.

Some examples of the most common ways for enterprises looking to strengthen their API security are listed as follows:

- Use tokens – Establish trusted identities and then control access to services and resources by using tokens assigned to those identities.

- Use encryption and signatures – Encrypt data using a method like TLS. Transport Layer Security is a cryptographic protocol designed to provide communications security over a computer network. Devices with signatures will ensure that the right users are decrypting and modifying the data.

- Upgrades and vulnerability identification – Enterprises need to upgrade their operating systems, networks, drivers, and API components periodically. They need to know how everything works together and identify weak spots that could be used to break into APIs. Some enterprises use sniffers to detect security issues and track data leaks. Sniffing is a process of monitoring and capturing all data packets passing through a given network.

- Use quotas and throttling – Often, enterprises need to set quotas on how often their API can be called and track its use over history. More calls on an API may indicate that it is being abused. It could also be a programming mistake, such as calling the API in an endless loop. Enterprises need to make rules for throttling to protect APIs from spikes and denial-of-service attacks.

- Use an API Gateway – It is also recommended to have an API Gateway as the major point of enforcement for API traffic. A good Gateway will allow to authenticate traffic as well as control and analyze how APIs are used.

Smart IoT Gateway Security

IoT Gateways are a solution to enable communication with devices irrespective of their protocols and also act as security agents for resource-constrained IoT devices, sensors, and actuators that lack the CPU horsepower, battery life, and storage to handle complex cryptographic security functions, such as secured access authentication and encryption. However, in an IoT environment, not only the devices but the Gateway itself is prone to various security threats since Gateways are exposed to the Internet. If the Gateway is not secured, all accompanying security technologies would become useless if the Gateways are compromised. Enterprises need to ensure that they deploy Smart IoT Gateways, which have foolproof security controls, and at a minimum the Gateways have endpoint security controls such as identity and access control, over-the-air updates, and threat detection feature.

Identity and Access Control (IAC)

Identity management and access control is the discipline of managing access to enterprise resources to keep systems and data secure. As a key component of the security architecture, IAC helps verify device or user identities before granting them the right level of access to systems and data.

The Gateway needs a root of trust to identify itself on the network before it can participate in data exchange. A Gateway should be designed as a trust anchor and equipped with key-based access control to grant access to authorized users and devices. To protect the secrets (keys and certificates), secured storage should be implemented.

Often, Gateways are exposed to extreme outdoor environments. Tamper-resistant hardware can protect them from physical damage.

Over-the-Air Updates and Secure Boot

Over-the-air updates ensure that the Gateway is running the latest software and firmware free from common vulnerabilities and exposures. Secure boot enables the Gateway to boot firmware images whose integrity and authenticity have been cryptographically verified. This precaution prevents booting the Gateway with malicious firmware.

Visibility and Threat Detection

Fine-grained event logging provides sufficient visibility into the processes running in the Gateway, which is useful for security audits and also automates threat detection and troubleshooting. In IoT environments, where accessibility could be constrained, it is more practical to automate threat detection by using machine learning or Artificial Intelligence. Machine learning enables enterprises to identify behavioral baselines and detect or even prevent anomalies, and such features should be validated before choosing an IoT Gateway.

Patch Management/Continuous Software Updates

Providing means of updating devices and software either over network connections or through automation is critical. Having a coordinated disclosure of vulnerabilities is also important to updating devices as soon as possible. Consider end-of-life strategies as well.

Hardware Security

Endpoint hardening includes making devices tamper-proof or tamper evident. This is especially important when devices will be used in harsh environments or where they will not be monitored physically.

IoT Platform Security

Almost all large IoT Platform vendors, such as AWS, Google, or Azure, have secured their platforms with the most comprehensive security postures and have built-in protection at the platform level. These platforms are built on a secure and proven cloud infrastructure and scale to billions of devices and trillions of messages.

Enterprises utilizing these products need to ensure that security features provided by these vendors are fully utilized to serve their IoT ecosystem.

Securing IoT Using Blockchain

A blockchain is a distributed ledger, similar to a database, but rather than being controlled by a central authority (i.e., a firm like Google, small company, or individual), the ledger is dispersed across multiple computers, which can be located all over the world and run by anyone with an Internet connection.

We will discuss in Chapter 9 about using blockchain for making a business impact rather than from a cyber security angle. However, Blockchain does offer an intriguing solution for IoT security as well. Blockchain contains strong protections against data tampering, locking access to Internet of Things devices, and allowing compromised devices in an IoT network to be shut down. However, IoT-blockchain technology is now in its initial stages, and a few major technology companies have begun to seek opportunities in this space. For example, the IBM Blockchain Platform allows enterprises to extend blockchain into cognitive IoT, a set of technologies that combines IoT and cognitive computing.

The adoption of IoT-blockchain technology is not yet widespread due to technical concerns and operational challenges. Scalability and storage are major issues in blockchain systems that maintain a large centralized ledger, and storing the ledger on edge nodes is considered inefficient since devices are not yet capable of storing large volumes of data or handling relatively large amounts of computational power. These factors are some of the challenges for shifting IoT networks onto blockchain platforms.

Though the concept is still in its infancy, it is likely to have a massive impact in the coming years. The implementation of standard security rules and regulations will encourage the adoption of IoT-blockchain technology. By introducing new standards of data privacy and peer-to-peer communication, blockchain can add a new degree of security to the Internet-enabled devices. Peer-to-peer communication refers to the transmission between two peer devices or systems over a network.

Because of these reasons, enterprises that have embarked on their IoT journey should adopt security by design principles to secure their IoT ecosystem rather than using blockchain.

Summary

This chapter is about security. We discussed that traditionally OT systems have not considered cyber security while designing and implementing their systems. However, with IoT, IT and OT systems are coming together, and hence cyber securing both IT and OT becomes extremely important.

We spoke about the importance of security by design in IoT, which is the inclusion of security design principles, technology, and governance at every stage of the IoT journey and within all layers of the IoT Standards Reference Model.

159

The first aspect of security by design is to procure devices which are built with security features such as multifactor authentication or biometrics. The second element is securing the application programming interfaces (APIs) – it is essential for enterprises to protect the integrity of data being sent from IoT devices to Smart IoT Gateways and the IoT Cloud Platform or back-end systems and ensure only authorized devices and applications communicate with APIs. Using a standard secured API Gateway is one of the best ways to secure APIs. The last aspect we discussed is that enterprises should deploy Smart IoT Gateways, which have foolproof security controls, and at a minimum the Gateways have endpoint security controls such as identity and access control, over-the-air updates, and threat detection feature. Similarly, enterprises need to deploy the IoT Cloud Platform with built-in security features.

In the next chapter, we will understand about Blockchain in detail and how it is beneficial for IoT use cases. We will also discuss about the different blockchain patterns that enterprises can utilize for their IoT use case implementation.

PART III

AI and Blockchain As Enablers for IoT

This part of the book discusses about the importance of Artificial Intelligence and Blockchain for IoT use cases.

We will discuss the importance of using a private blockchain for IoT use cases along with the five IoT-Blockchain implementation patterns, using which enterprises can enable seamless communication between IoT devices, Smart IoT Gateways, and IoT platforms to blockchain.

Artificial Intelligence is one of the very important features within an IoT Standards Reference Model. The reference model recommends applying AI patterns to generate insights from data and take appropriate actions automatically. The chapter will also provide a perspective on how and when to apply AI in an IoT context.

CHAPTER 9

Blockchain with IoT

Blockchain is one of the interesting topics in the technology circles which is currently revolutionizing the way enterprises will do business in the future. Though the technology is still in the experimental stage, there are a lot of benefits which many enterprises are already achieving in part from the technology. Discussing the basics, Blockchain was developed as a technology to exchange money by some young mathematicians, and now this has come to the center stage where almost every business transaction can be executed securely and cost-effectively. Blockchains promise to bring collaboration between companies, enabling the sharing of both factual data and business logic across an ecosystem in a standardized, structured, and secure manner.

Blockchain is a shared cryptographically unalterable ledger for recording the history of transactions. Cryptography is associated with the process of converting ordinary plain text into unintelligible text and vice versa. It is a method of storing and transmitting data in a particular form so that only those for whom it is intended can read and process it.

Blockchain is not centralized, which is the most interesting part – what this means is that it is not owned by one party or person. It is democratized, which is the important thing, and because of this it increases trust between parties because no single entity owns the blockchain. It increases accountability (since every authorized party is part of the decision-making process) and above all transparency (since every authorized party can see each and every transaction). With such transparency and accountability, the technology enables a much lower friction.

© Venkatesh Upadrista 2021
V. Upadrista, *IoT Standards with Blockchain*,
https://doi.org/10.1007/978-1-4842-7271-8_9

Let me explain about blockchain in a simple language.

You can consider blockchain as a book. A book has many pages, and all pages are glued with a binder. The book is owned by one person or in some cases owned by multiple people. Each page has multiple entries or transactions – such as person A holds X value, person B has Y value – and each of these transactions is used to compute a unique value, which is called a unique identifier, for the page. So this means that if any value in the page changes, the unique identifier will also change.

In blockchain language, a book is called a ledger, pages are called the blocks, and the binder is the chain of a blockchain. If the book is owned and managed by one person, it is called a centralized ledger management, and if the book is owned and managed by multiple people, it is called a distributed ledger management. The unique identifier is called the hash. If anything in the block changes, the hash value changes since the hash is generated using each entry in the block. One of the important features of a blockchain is immutability, which means that any transaction once recorded cannot be altered. If someone tries to tamper or change the content of an existing block, the changes will reflect only in their copy, and the rest will still continue to see the untampered version of the block, which means the blockchain is immutable. This makes a blockchain tamper-proof and highly secure. Now adding a new block to a blockchain is similar to adding a new page to the book. This is what blockchain is all about.

There are two variants of blockchain. One is called the Public Blockchain, and another is called the Private Blockchain.

Public Blockchain

A public blockchain is a blockchain network where anyone can join whenever they want. Basically, there are no restrictions when it comes to participation. More so, anyone can see the ledger and take part in the process. For example, Ethereum is one of the public blockchain platforms.

If enterprises are looking for a fully decentralized network system, then public blockchain is the way to go. However, a public blockchain can become very problematic when enterprises try to incorporate a public blockchain network with the enterprise internal blockchain process.

The best part about public blockchains is the concept which says that all the participants have equal rights. Everyone can see the ledger as well, thus maintaining transparency at all times. However, public blockchains do come with their fair share of flaws as well. In reality, these platforms are slower than usual; they are less secure and many times violate data privacy laws. Furthermore, it can attract malicious people using the platform for illegal activities because of the anonymous nature.

Though public blockchains have their own share of benefits, enterprises typically tend to adopt private blockchains to run their businesses. More importantly in an IoT and AI context, private blockchains are the most popular and recommended model.

So in simple terms, a public blockchain follows a distributed ledger management instead of a centralized ledger. In a centralized ledger, one person or entity is in charge of the blockchain, and in a distributed ledger, all individuals or entities who participate in the blockchain get a copy of the complete ledger and are responsible for the ledger.

In a public blockchain environment, anyone can add a new block to a blockchain, but they have to solve a very complex puzzle. The issue with this approach is that solving a puzzle consumes a lot of compute power.

Private Blockchain

A private blockchain is a special type of blockchain technology where only a single organization or a consortium of organizations has authority over the network. The network is not open for the public people to join in. All the private blockchain solutions will have some form of authorization scheme to identity which entity is entering the platform.

A private blockchain network requires an invitation and must be validated by either the network starter or by a set of rules put in place by the network starter. Businesses that set up a private blockchain will generally set up a permissioned network. This places restrictions on who is allowed to participate in the network and who can perform which transaction. Participants need to obtain an invitation or permission to join. The access control mechanism could vary – existing participants could decide future entrants, or a regulatory authority could issue licenses for participation, or a consortium could make the decisions instead. Once an entity has joined the network, it will play a role in maintaining the blockchain in a decentralized manner.

In a private blockchain environment, enterprises do not need to spend compute power to add a new block to the blockchain since the network starter or business owner can add a block to the blockchain.

In a typical scenario, if we look at any enterprise business end to end, it is an amalgamation of multiple parties communicating with each other to complete a business transaction or a business process as depicted in Figure 9-1.

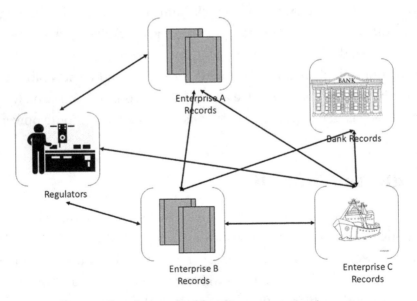

Figure 9-1. *Example of a typical business transaction*

There are producers, the finance, regulators, transport agencies, and retailers, and each of these parties uses their own systems to maintain their records and communicates with others based on these records. As this communication and recording process becomes complex, there can be several disagreements, and to prove correctness of their own data and records, enterprises spend millions of dollars on intermediaries, audits and compliance, and so on. This is the reality of today, which means an inefficient system, and the main reason for this inefficiency is because each entity within our economy maintains their own records, and in many cases these records are not shared or are made transparent with other entities. Private Blockchain is a solution to address this inefficiency in the current economy for businesses to transact and communicate with each other.

Hyperledger

A blockchain is a single database that is shared with every enterprise which is directly or indirectly connected to the business, and every enterprise has an identical copy of every transaction that is part of the blockchain.

One of the concepts that comes up often when we speak about blockchains is Hyperledger. Hyperledger is an umbrella project of open source blockchains and related tools, started in December 2015 by the Linux Foundation, and has received contributions from IBM, Intel, and SAP to support the collaborative development of blockchain-based distributed ledgers.

Hyperledger is a global enterprise blockchain project that offers the necessary framework, standards, guidelines, and tools to build open source blockchains and related applications for use across various industries. Hyperledger is a permissioned blockchain which is designed specifically for enterprises to do business using a blockchain. It is an environment in which every one of the parties who agreed to be part of the consortium in the permission chain gets visibility to all of the data that they have permission, which gives them the ability to see every allowed transaction that is registered on the blockchain. As an example, a retailer will be able to see where their products are; even though it is delivered by a third-party logistic company, they can find the location, condition of their shipments or products, and so on. Since the chain is not controlled by one person, there would be no disagreements, and no one can tamper the data – there is just one state of truth which is distributed and transparent across every member, and every member has the same priority and accountability as others on the data and transactions. And whatever has been entered once becomes permanent, which means there is no debate or question on the accuracy of the data.

A cryptocurrency, broadly defined, is a currency that takes the form of tokens or "coins" and exists on a distributed and decentralized ledger powered by Blockchain.

A smart contract is a self-executing contract with the terms of the agreement between the buyer and the seller being directly written into lines of code. The code and the agreements contained therein exist across a distributed, decentralized blockchain network.

Blockchain Benefits Almost Every Industry Today

With an initial purpose of a mechanism behind cryptocurrencies, today the blockchain technology has stepped far beyond just powering the bitcoin transactions. Blockchain is a powerful and secure technology that is getting into almost every industry, from banking or medicine to even the government sector. Combined with IoT, blockchain is redefining the way in which enterprises can do business in future.

For example, in shipping and logistics, let us consider one of the trade scenarios where each item becomes trackable starting from the point of production to delivery via ships or trucks and finally reaching the warehouse and then to the store. If every enterprise part of the supply chain, such as the producer of the item, the freight management company which is transporting the products, the warehouse which stores the products, and the retailer who finally sells the products, is able to track where the items are at any point in time, the condition of the items, and who is currently in charge, it makes the whole end-to-end supply chain very transparent and effective.

Let us discuss another case study, about how food moves from farm to fork and how blockchain could be a disruptive technology to make that safer and sustainable.

You might have heard of a salmonella-tainted outbreak that occurred in 2018 in the United States by a company called Peanut Corporation of America which has killed 9 people and more than 700 reported cases of salmonella poisoning in 46 states. This company produced a very small volume of peanut paste in the United States, tune to just 2%. Peanut paste is an ingredient that is used in a lot of products. Because a lot of products use this butter, during the outbreak almost every product which uses this ingredient was deemed contaminated. The chain reaction was that anything that had granulated peanut from any supplier got recalled, and the products ranged from crackers, chocolate bars and cookies, ice creams, and even pet food products. There were a total of 3913 different food products that had to be recalled, and this was just because a small manufacturer that produced 2% of peanut butter shipped salmonella-tainted peanut butter. The CEO of the company Stewart Parnell was awarded several years of imprisonment for doing that. Some of these recalls that happened took as long as two months after the initial outbreak was detected. Can you imagine for two months contaminated products sitting on shelves, because people did not know that a contaminated

169

ingredient was in their products? And this is not unique to the United States, there are several such outbreaks in Asia and Europe as well.

The key is to understand what solutions exist that can overcome such kind of fiascos – IoT combined with blockchain is the solution. There is a need to have a system in place that can provide a fully transparent and digitized view on the food system, based on which in the preceding case study only those products that get affected could be recalled.

Let us take another example of farm to fork for a simple sliced mango or apple. Mangoes are generally grown by small farmers somewhere in Central or South America.

A mango tree is planted from seed and requires five to eight years before it will bear fruits. Once a tree bears some fruit, they are harvested before they are fully ripened, which takes one to two weeks. Once they are ripened, mangoes get transported by air, land, or sea, and in many cases, they are transported cross country where they are cleared by customs, and then mangoes are brought to the processing facility of the retail stores where they are cleaned and then finally sliced and put on the shelves for sales by retailers.

When a customer enters a store, they are not aware of the lengthy process of who harvested the mangoes, in what conditions the mangoes were transported, and how they arrived at the store. It is a complicated journey. However, from a food safety perspective, it is very important to know each and every step in the process starting from farm to fork, especially when something like the peanut butter fiasco happens. Today, it takes days to trace any food product from a grocery cart to the farm, and most of this traceability today is achieved using disparate methods across the life cycle, and in many cases, this is recorded on paper.

A combination of IoT and Blockchain can overcome this traditional challenge by bringing in a full traceability into the process, and such level of traceability can be achieved in minutes. The solution can move beyond traceability to transparency, which is one of the most important aspects in a food safety–regulated industry.

Traceability has the following attributes: the three Ws – what, when, and where. This is a mango, where did this come from, where did this go and at what time, where was it in on these dates, and so on. Using the current systems, one can never achieve an end-to-end view of the complete farm to fork system.

What is envisioned with transparency is that enterprises can have an entire interconnected view of that system. Transparency attributes are how was it produced, were any pesticides used to harvest the product or was it organically grown, and so on.

With IoT and blockchain, enterprises can achieve both transparency and traceability together. There can be IoT sensors that can be deployed at the farms, at the packaging houses, and at the distribution centers that can track and trace the items from farm to fork, and all this data can be secured using blockchain technology where all parties who are part of the supply chain can participate in the process. Using this model, enterprises can go to an extent where customers will be able to scan a QR code on a package and know where that product came from, how it was preserved and at what temperature, how much chemicals were used during production, and any other attributes that they choose.

And lastly, such a system brings in a lot of customer trust on companies and the whole food systems.

IoT Blockchain Implementation Patterns

So far, we have spoken about the importance of blockchain and the different use cases which make blockchain a powerful technology in an IoT context. However, with different challenges we have in IoT, such as legacy devices and protocols, enormous data generated by these devices, along with a wide variety of IoT tools and technologies in the market, applying blockchain in IoT use cases needs to be carefully planned.

The Industrial Internet Consortium (IIC) was formed to accelerate the development, adoption, and widespread use of interconnected machines and devices and intelligent analytics. IIC has defined four patterns[1] of communication between IoT devices, Smart IoT Gateways, and IoT platforms to blockchain based on certain simple guidelines as depicted in Figure 9-2. A fifth pattern has been added as part of IoT Standards that helps achieve interoperability when applying Blockchain to IoT.

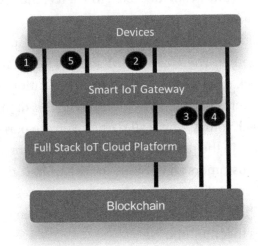

Figure 9-2. *IoT Blockchain patterns*

Pattern 1: Device ➤ IoT Cloud Platform ➤ Blockchain

This pattern focuses on the IoT devices that have Wi-Fi and/or cellular connectivity and are able to directly communicate with the IoT cloud platform using various IoT data protocols. In this pattern, the IoT cloud manages all the device data, and the blockchain serves as the data integrity

---

[1] https://hub.iiconsortium.org/portal/IndividualContribution/5db03a83f 7679b000f0e762f

layer. The IoT cloud platform chooses which data and events will be stored in the blockchain.

Pattern 2: Device ➤ IoT Gateway ➤ IoT Cloud Platform ➤ Blockchain

This pattern is defined specifically for resource-constrained IoT devices (e.g., sensors, RFIDs, smart meters, etc.) that can only connect to an IoT Gateway via low-power wireless communication protocols (e.g., Zigbee, Z-Wave, LoRa, etc.), which then forward the collected data to the IoT cloud platform. The blockchain in this pattern plays the same role as that in pattern 1.

Pattern 3: Device ➤ IoT Gateway ➤ Blockchain

This pattern is aimed for heavy edge computing use cases where the IoT Gateway directly handles the connection, storage, processing, and analysis in a distributed manner. In this pattern, the blockchain replaces the IoT cloud platform for controlling and managing IoT devices and Gateways to realize various asset-related core functionalities.

Pattern 4: Device ➤ Blockchain

This pattern mainly targets machine-to-machine communication and payment scenarios, where the IoT devices, which are equipped with Wi-Fi/cellular modules, need to communicate with others in a decentralized manner. Smart contracts are extensively utilized in this pattern to define the interaction rules and policies between IoT devices. The IoT devices monitor the specific events on the blockchain and take actions accordingly.

Pattern 5: Device ➤ IoT Gateway ➤ IoT Platform

Pattern 5 has been introduced as part of the IoT Standards Reference Model which does not include communication with blockchain. This is a pattern which mandatory needs to coexist with one of the four patterns we discussed about for any IoT use case implementation following the IoT Standards Reference Model. The reason why this pattern is introduced is to make enterprises understand that not every transaction and not every data generated by the IoT device needs to be recorded on the blockchain, else there would be a massive data explosion. There are very few use cases where patterns 1–4 can be applied in silos, and such use cases need to be identified very carefully.

Apply Integration Patterns Wisely

With the introduction of blockchain, there is more trust in the overall network; however, it is not essential that all data that is generated by the IoT devices and transactions needs to be recorded on the blockchain, and this is one of the reasons why pattern 5 has been introduced. It is very essential to understand what needs to be recorded on the blockchain and what can still directly reside either on the IoT Cloud Platform or on the Smart IoT Gateways.

Pattern 4 combined with 5 (called pattern 45) is a widely used pattern where a machine-to-machine communication is required. To apply this pattern, it is mandatory that devices are able to connect to the Internet and should have compute capability. This pattern is applied in connected car technology where a car manufactured by one company needs to communicate with a car of another company, or an electronic payment needs to be initiated by machines, for example, when an electric car uses a charging station, the car automatically makes payment to the charging station without any human intervention.

Pattern 45 can also be applied in much simpler use cases, such as home camera security systems. Home camera security systems are used to monitor and alert on different kinds of events, such as unauthorized entries or burglary. However, most of the existing home camera systems have not been designed to handle cyber-attacks, and therefore we always see news in the media reporting different types of attacks on the home systems.

Credential stuffing is a type of cyber-attack where stolen account credentials, typically consisting of lists of usernames and/or email addresses and the corresponding passwords, are used to gain unauthorized access to user accounts through large-scale automated login requests directed against a web application.

Multifactor authentication is an electronic authentication method in which a computer user is granted access to a website or application only after successfully presenting two or more pieces of evidence to an authentication mechanism: knowledge, possession, and inherence.

When we analyze the cyber security attacks against the home camera, there are many security concerns:

- The first is the hacking of usernames and passwords. Many home camera systems use traditional username- and password-based logging solutions without a multifactor authentication. Such lapses are easy prey for hackers, which lead to attacks such as credential stuffing.

- The second security concern is called the database
  breaches where password leakage and ownership
  compromise take place by hacking the database of the
  home security systems.

- The third type of attack is called the insecure device
  binding, where hackers take over the camera
  ownership by posing as genuine owners.

- And lastly, data integrity for local or cloud storage is
  also a breach which is mostly heard on home cameras.
  What this means is that hackers can enter the local
  storage such as SD cards or remote storage such as
  cloud where video files are stored. In this type of attack,
  data can be tampered, such as inserting new clips or
  deleting and modifying existing video clips.

With the introduction of blockchain pattern 45, such kind of attacks
can be fully eliminated. As an example, one solution is to replace the
traditional username- and password-based logging with a passwordless
solution using Blockchain, where devices and homeowners can participate
in the blockchain to enable a hackproof communication. Another example
is called blockchain-based ownership management. In this solution, a
blockchain address (unique identifier) is generated to recognize the owner
of the device when the camera is first turned on, and a foolproof pairing
is enabled between the device owner and the home security systems
on the blockchain. In this solution, device ownership is protected using
blockchain technology instead of a centralized server.

In a smart factory kind of use case, pattern 2 combined with 5 (pattern 25)
and pattern 3 combined with 5 (pattern 35) are mostly widely used since there
are many legacy devices in a factory setting that cannot communicate to the
IoT cloud platform or blockchain directly.

Another industry where pattern 35 is most widely used is the healthcare sector. IoT in healthcare is called IoMT, which stands for the Internet of Medical Things. I have come across many enterprises that have chosen pattern 1, some using blockchain and many others without a blockchain for their IoMT implementation because it looks quite easy to implement. However, these enterprises will either need to rearchitect and modernize their IoT systems in near future or may have already started on this journey. Pattern 1 is not the right pattern if enterprises are looking for a scalable IoMT solution. Some have argued that Fast Healthcare Interoperability Resources (FHIR) has been adopted as a standard in the health industry, and almost all device manufacturers are utilizing this standard during the device manufacturing process. Therefore, utilizing pattern 1 should not be a problem. I personally contradict such a statement, and we will discuss why adopting pattern 1 is a road to failure in the subsequent discussion.

Fast Healthcare Interoperability Resources (FHIR) is the global industry standard for passing healthcare data between systems. FHIR defines how healthcare information can be exchanged between different computer systems regardless of how it is stored in those systems. FHIR is based on Internet standards widely used by healthcare. In healthcare, there are several classes of medical devices.

One class of devices deals with patients for remote patient monitoring (RPM) – RPM is the most common application for healthcare where IoT devices automatically collect health metrics like heart rate, blood pressure, temperature, and more from patients who are not physically present in a healthcare facility, eliminating the need for patients to travel to the hospitals. Data is then forwarded to healthcare professionals and/or patients for the next steps. These are devices such as Fitbit and Apple Watch that an individual can wear all the time, and these devices are passively monitoring activities and transmit patient data for processing or analysis.

There are other class of devices that are ambient, such as sensors that exist in hospital beds or devices to monitor a room temperature or monitor a patient behavior. And these devices take medical readings or reports on patient behavior.

And then there are other class of devices that are ingestible monitoring medical devices which are small pill-like sensors which measure pH (potential hydrogen), temperature, and pressure or monitor whether or not patients have taken their medicines.

The above is a subset of several classes and hundreds of devices that are present in the healthcare industry and range from very small devices with minimal processing power to large devices with ample data storage and processing power.

Building Blocks for IoMT and Associated Challenges

Ingestion of Data

Not all devices can send data at high frequency. Some devices just run reading once a day, and there are others which produce data at extremely high rates, such as every second and even subsecond. Enterprises need to design a standard solution that will be able to interact with both these class of devices. Patterns 25 and 45 could be the right choice here.

Latency

The challenge with certain class of devices in the medical world is that they run on batteries, and data processing at the device level causes latency issues. Patterns 25 and 35 could be the right choice here.

Number of Devices

There are a multitude of devices in a health ecosystem without much standardization, and each device reports data in their own unique way. Pattern 25 could be the right choice here.

Interoperability

One of the biggest challenges in the health industry with IoT devices is that most of the devices do not interoperate with others. And this is the key factor that needs to be accounted for when implementing use cases in IoMT. FHIR is becoming a common standard across the healthcare sector and provides a standardized way of sharing data across multiple hospital systems; however, the standard is still evolving, and not many legacy devices have adopted this standard. Pattern 25 could be the right choice here.

Late Arrival of Data

One of the major challenges I have come across in IoMT use cases is the late arriving data from devices (as an example with wearable devices), since most of these devices use a Gateway for Internet connection, for example, smartphones. These devices collect data for hours or even days sometimes, and once an Internet connectivity is established, data is then sent to the back-end systems. So, the first challenge in such a scenario is that systems should be able to handle the burst of data, and second is that the systems should be able to make sense of the data and associate it with the right time period.

So far, there is no real standard that has been defined on how the devices should send data, and therefore each device manufacturer has defined their own standards. So, if a device is collecting data offline, some may send the most recent data first, and some may send old data first. This means that the IoMT solutions should address this challenge. This makes pattern 1 highly inefficient since device software needs to be rewritten to embed such standards. Patterns 25 and 35 are most relevant in this scenario.

Data Duplication

The second major challenge faced in an IoMT context is data duplication. The way in which devices choose to resend data during anticipated failures is different for different devices since there is no standard defined. Some devices choose to resend complete data again because they were in the middle of transmitting data when a connection was lost, or they did not get an acknowledgment that a particular piece of data was successfully received. Irrespective of the reasons, since each device operates differently without a standard mechanism, it becomes a challenge when a multitude of different devices come together. Patterns 25 and 35 are the most relevant in this scenario.

Data Formats

In addition to data duplication and late data arrival, IoT devices have their own way of representing data, and there is no clear standardization. The data captured by IoT devices is produced in a mix of data formats, including structured, semistructured, and unstructured data.

With the magnitude of standardization challenges that IoT devices pose in the medical industry, if enterprises try to create solutions at the device level using pattern 1, it is obvious that managing and maintaining these devices not only brings in a lot of OPEX costs but there will be massive CAPEX costs. CAPEX costs will be toward making the devices adapt to a standard way of operations, and this may mean rewriting or upgrading software on these devices. OPEX costs will be for patches and upgrades. Cost is one part, but there are other challenges, such as devices using different communication protocols to talk to the external world, which will need a solution. All these challenges make pattern 1 inappropriate in an IoMT context. By using pattern 35, devices can be left as it is, and an IoT Gateway will address these challenges at the Gateway level. There are several commercial-grade IoT Gateways that have already addressed these challenges, and therefore pattern 35 is considered the most appropriate in large-scale IoMT use cases.

Summary

Blockchain is a shared cryptographically unalterable ledger for recording the history of transactions. In this chapter, we understood how blockchain works and the different types of blockchains, such as private and public blockchains:

- A private blockchain is a technology where only a single organization or a consortium of organizations has authority over the network. The network is not open for the public people to join in and is the preferred one for IoT use cases.

- A public blockchain is a blockchain network where anyone can join whenever they want. There are no restrictions when it comes to participation.

We subsequently discussed how Blockchain powers IoT use cases with several examples and case studies by utilizing the five types of Blockchain IoT patterns which enterprises can choose based on their use cases:

1. In the first pattern, devices communicate with the IoT Cloud Platform which in turn communicates with Blockchain.

2. In the second pattern, devices communicate with the Smart IoT Gateway. The Gateway then communicates with the IoT Cloud Platform which in turn communicates with Blockchain.

3. The third pattern is where devices communicate directly with the Smart IoT Gateway which in turn communicates with Blockchain.

4. In the fourth pattern, devices communicate directly with Blockchain.

5. In the fifth pattern, devices communicate with the Smart IoT Gateway. The Gateway then communicates with the IoT Cloud Platform. No blockchain interaction in this pattern.

In the next chapter, we will discuss about applying Artificial Intelligence in IoT.

CHAPTER 10

Artificial Intelligence in the IoT World (Applied IoT)

Automation is the application of machines to tasks once performed by human beings. Although the term mechanization is often used to refer to the simple replacement of human labor by machines, automation generally implies the integration of machines into a self-governing system. Automation has revolutionized those areas in which it has been introduced, and there is scarcely an aspect of modern life that has been unaffected by it.

Digital transformation and automation go hand in hand. Digital transformation is the act of harmonizing business processes with current, automation-based technology to make the entire breadth of cross-enterprise workflows convenient, optimized, and less erroneous. In other words, it shifts tasks from being siloed, department specific, and manually done to being streamlined, universally accessible, and strategically automated. It does this by introducing new software to the current systems. This software acts as an extension of those already in place, performing many of the repetitive and monotonous functions that would have previously fallen on multiple employees across multiple departments. Such was the main cause of business process lag times and chokepoints

© Venkatesh Upadrista 2021
V. Upadrista, *IoT Standards with Blockchain*,
https://doi.org/10.1007/978-1-4842-7271-8_10

as parts of that workflow stalled between departmental queues. However, with digital transformation technologies in place, employees need to spend less doing things "the old way." Bolstered by automated technology and streamlined, cross-department software, enterprises can now divert attention onto higher-level, high-order work, resulting in a fine-tuned enterprise workflow process that minimizes waste and maximizes resource productivity.

The world is moving toward automation, and there is no technical limitation on how much automation can be done in an enterprise. However, the benefits achieved from automation vis-à-vis the cost incurred on automation always need to be analyzed before making a decision. In simple terms, tasks which are highly repeatable need to be automated.

There are different tools and technologies that enable automation. Robotic process automation (RPA) is one such technology and is the term used for software tools that partially or fully automate human activities that are manual, rule based, and repetitive. They work by replicating the actions of an actual human interacting with one or more software applications to perform tasks, such as data entry, process standard transactions, or respond to simple customer service queries.

Robotic process automation tools are not replacements for the underlying business applications; rather, they simply automate the already manual tasks of human workers.

One of the key benefits of robotic process automation is that the tools do not alter existing systems or infrastructure. Traditional automation tools and technologies used to interact with systems using application programming interfaces (APIs), which means writing code which can lead to concerns about quality assurance, maintaining that code, and responding to changes in the underlying applications.

With robotic process automation, scripting or programming needs to be performed for automating a repetitive task for which a subject matter expert (SME) is required who understands how the work is done manually. In addition, the data sources and destinations need to be highly structured and unchanging – robotic process automation tools cannot apply intelligence to deal with errors or exceptions at all. But even with these considerations, there are tangible, concrete benefits from robotic process automation. Studies by the London School of Economics suggest RPA can deliver a potential return on investment of between 30% and 200% – and that is just in the first year.[1] Savings on this scale will prove hard to resist. Last year, Deloitte found that while only 9% of surveyed companies had implemented RPA, almost 74% planned to investigate the technology in the next 12 months.

The limitation of RPA is that they mimic human behavior in a static way, and they lack a human's ability or intelligence to adapt to change. Artificial Intelligence is the next big technology that complements RPA by making it possible for machines to mimic humans in functions such as learning and problem-solving. Artificial Intelligence could learn from the past data and perform tasks in much more intelligent way as compared to RPA which can perform only repetitive tasks.

RPA and Artificial Intelligence are coming together, and the cost savings and benefits are too compelling for companies to ignore. Robotic process automation (RPA), for example, can capture and interpret the actions of existing business process applications, such as claims processing or customer support. Once the "robot software" understands these tasks, it can take over running them, and it does so far more quickly, accurately, and tirelessly than any human. Complementing RPA with AI algorithms can provide additional benefit that the robot can learn from data and from its mistakes so that it can improve its accuracy and performance over the period of time.

Applicability of RPA and AI combination can span in improving cost as well as bringing new insights to the business based on which intelligent

---

[1] Leslie Willcocks, professor of technology, work, and globalization at the London School of Economics' department of management. Source: McKinsey.com, December 2016

decisions can be made. A combination of RPA and Artificial Intelligence can provide maximum automation capabilities for enterprises and is one of the most important elements to be considered during digital transformation. These benefits are amplified further in an IoT context, which we will discuss in subsequent sections. Combining IoT with AI can create "smart machines" that simulate intelligent behavior to make well-informed decisions with little or no human intervention. The result is an acceleration in innovation which can significantly boost productivity for the enterprises involved. IoT and AI markets are developing rapidly and in tandem.

Robotic Process Automation

As discussed, robotic process automation (RPA) is a technology that allows to configure computer software or a "robot" to emulate and integrate the actions of a human interacting within digital systems to execute a business process. RPA utilizes the user interface to capture data and manipulate applications just like humans do. They interpret, trigger responses, and communicate with other systems in order to perform a vast variety of repetitive tasks.

Many enterprises are turning to RPA to streamline enterprise operations and reduce costs. With RPA, businesses can automate mundane rules-based business processes, enabling business users to devote more time to serving customers or other higher-value work. RPA bots called virtual IT support teams are replacing humans on repetitive mundane processes. Enterprises further are also supercharging their automation efforts by injecting RPA with cognitive technologies such as machine learning, speech recognition, and natural language processing, automating higher-order tasks that in the past required the perceptual and judgment capabilities of humans. This is called Artificial Intelligence.

The key difference that distinguishes RPA from enterprise automation tools like business process management (BPM) is that RPA uses software or cognitive robots to perform and optimize process operations rather than human operators. Unlike BPM, RPA is a quick and highly effective fix that does not require invasive integration or changes to underlying systems, allowing organizations to rapidly deliver efficiencies and cost savings mainly by replacing humans with software "robots."

RPA is great for automation, but there are limitations which need to be kept in mind. As an example, because RPA usually interacts with user interfaces, even minor changes to those interfaces may lead to a broken process.

Artificial Intelligence

Artificial Intelligence (AI) is the "science of making machines smart." Today, we can teach machines to be like humans. We can give them the ability to see, hear, speak, write, and move.

AI is a broad term that covers many subfields that aim to build machines that can do things which require intelligence when done by humans. These subfields are depicted in Figure 10-1 and are listed as follows:

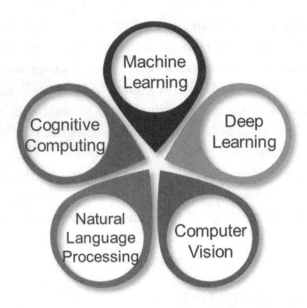

Figure 10-1. *AI subfields*

Machine learning – Machine learning provides systems the ability to automatically learn and improve from experience without being explicitly programmed. It focuses on the development of computer programs that can access data and use it to learn for themselves. Machine learning is the ability of computer systems to improve their performance by exposure to data without the need to follow explicitly programmed instructions. It is the process of automatically spotting patterns in large amounts of data that can then be used to make predictions.

Deep learning – This is a relatively new and hugely powerful technique that involves a family of algorithms that processes information in deep "neural" networks where the output from one layer becomes the input for the next one. Neural networks are computing systems vaguely inspired by the biological neural networks that constitute animal brains. The data structures and functionality of neural networks are designed to simulate associative memory. Deep learning algorithms have proved hugely successful in, for example, detecting cancerous cells or forecasting disease but with one huge caveat: there is no way to identify which factors the deep learning program uses to reach its conclusion.

Computer vision – It is the ability of computers to identify objects, scenes, and activities in images using techniques to decompose the task of analyzing images into manageable pieces, detecting the edges and textures of objects in an image, and comparing images to known objects for classification.

Natural language/speech processing – It is the ability of computers to work with text and language the way humans do, for instance, extracting meaning from text/speech or even generating text that is readable, stylistically natural, and grammatically correct.

Cognitive computing – A relatively new term, favored by IBM, cognitive computing applies knowledge from cognitive science to build an architecture of multiple AI subsystems, including machine learning, natural language processing, vision, and human-computer interaction, to simulate human thought processes with the aim of making high-level decisions in complex situations. According to IBM, the aim is to help humans make better decisions, rather than making the decisions for them.

Data Science

IoT concepts have matured in the last few years and are continuing to mature. There has been a growing focus on the importance of security, analytics at the edge, and other technologies and platforms that are necessary to make IoT projects successful. However, one of the most important elements that is necessary for an IoT use case to deliver results is data. In fact, one important element that is missing from the phrase "Internet of Things" is perhaps the most important piece of the puzzle – the data itself.

IoT is all about data. Almost all enterprises are out there collecting huge amounts of data to make business decisions based on this data. The more data enterprises have, the more business insights they can generate. Using data science, enterprises uncover patterns in data that they did not even know existed. For example, one can discover that they are at risk of an accident based on the data which another car in front of them sends. Data science is being used extensively in such scenarios. Enterprises are using data science to build recommendation engines, predict machine behavior, and much more. All of this is only possible when enterprises have enough amount of data so that various algorithms could be applied on that data to give more accurate results. Data science is all about applying Artificial Intelligence using machine learning algorithms on huge data sets to make predictions and also to discover patterns in the data.

The Link Between Artificial Intelligence and Data Science

The link between data science and Artificial Intelligence is a one-to-one mapping as we discussed earlier. This means that data science helps AIs figure out solutions to problems by linking similar data for future use. Fundamentally, data science allows AIs to find appropriate and meaningful information from those huge pools of data faster and more efficiently. Without data science, AI does not exist. AI is a collection of technologies that excel at extracting insights and patterns from large sets of data, then making predictions based on that information.

An example is Facebook's facial recognition system which, over time, gathers a lot of data about existing users and applies the same techniques for facial recognition with new users. Another example is Google's self-driving car which gathers data from its surroundings in real time and processes this data to make intelligent decisions on the road.

A typical non-AI system relies on human inputs to work just like an accounting software. The system is hardcoded with rules manually. Then, it follows those rules exactly to help do the taxes. The system only improves if human programmers improve it. But machine learning tools can improve on their own. This improvement comes from a machine assessing its own performance based on new data.

Importance of Quality Data

The key to AI success is having a high-quality data. AI can provide superior results only if it can learn from superior and high-quality data very specific to the use case enterprises are automating using AI. As an example, to solve a physics problem, if you provide mathematics-related data to an AI system, then results would not be encouraging. Your systems will learn something, but efforts probably would not help the system answer your test questions correctly. Another example, if you train a computer vision system for autonomous vehicles with images of sidewalks mislabeled as streets, the results could be disastrous. In order to develop accurate results using machine learning algorithms, you will need high-quality training data. To generate high-quality data, you will need skilled annotators to carefully label the information you plan to use with your algorithm.

If data is not good, then AI will fail in providing the desired results, because AI uses machine learning to learn from the data, and therefore enterprises need quality data. If data is not good, AI systems will not learn good and therefore will not give good results. This means that organizations using AI must devote huge amounts of resources to ensuring they have sufficient amounts of high-quality data so that their AI tools are giving desired results. This does not necessarily mean that enterprises need a fully functional enterprise-level big data platform to embark their journey on Artificial Intelligence. Artificial Intelligence can work on a subset of quality data specific to the use case, and enterprises can create a data store that can cater to the specific use case and use this data to train systems.

Today, almost all products available in the market, irrespective of what the tool specializes in, claim to have AI features built in the tool, which has caused a lot of confusion in the technology market on which tools to use for AI-driven use cases. However, one needs to understand that almost all tools whose primary tool capability is not AI or machine learning provide only generic AI capabilities and can perform very limited AI tasks. If one needs to apply Artificial Intelligence within their enterprises across a broad spectrum of IoT use cases, then they need to look at IoT Cloud Platforms that can perform AI on IoT data for that specific use case. Azure IoT Platform is one such example.

Artificial Intelligence and IoT

We discussed in previous sections that RPA uses predefined rules to perform activities, and since the last few years, RPA has been highly successful for several use cases. Even if we consider some of the world's largest problems solved by organizations like NASA, it had been achieved with traditional rules or theories. As an example, for flying from Earth to Mars, NASA does not aim for where Mars is currently, it aims to find out where Mars will be nine months later, since it takes nine months for astronauts to travel from Earth to Mars. The rule which NASA applies to predict the location of Mars after nine months is based on the 300-year-old Newton's law of motion. Newton's theory works for all planets in our solar system, except Mercury. Mercury is another story anyways because it is too close to the sun, etc., and other reasons. A similar case is with the stock market. A predefined rule such as "buy stocks if the short-term average of the stock cuts over the long-term average of the stock" works quite well. Such predefined rules used to be the norm in the last few years when AI was not part of the enterprise strategy, which is not the case anymore. AI is becoming mainstream for most organizations, and there are more and more use cases that are proving the benefits of AI. Because of this renowned focus, enterprises have started moving away thinking about traditional rules and rule-based systems. The new norm is – give me data and I will create models by learning from the data, and the more I learn, the better the models I will create. This is what Artificial Intelligence is all about. For IoT use cases, Artificial Intelligence is amplifying benefits to such an extent that enterprises are able to exceed their profit margins, while many other enterprises are entering into new business domains which they never had thought about in the past.

IoT creates a lot of data. Devices send large volumes and varieties of information at high speed, which makes IoT data management very complex. We are going to discuss in detail about data management in IoT in Chapter 11. Managing such complex IoT data requires robust and tailored data architectures, policies, practices, and procedures that properly meet the IoT data life cycle needs. Traditional big data approaches and infrastructure are not sufficient, and enterprises need to validate how IoT Cloud Platforms or IoT Gateways are addressing IoT-specific data challenges during the evaluation process.

Scalability and agility is one of the biggest concerns when it comes to IoT data. The sheer size of IoT data traffic and its immediacy make data management complex for IoT use cases. Some of the key challenges which IoT Cloud Platforms or IoT Gateways need to address from an IoT data perspective are listed as follows:

- Given that the number of IoT devices will increase with time, say from 40 to 400,000 devices, how will IoT data architecture accommodate this?

- Most of the IoT data has a short shelf life – this means that actions need to be taken right after devices generate the data. As an example, if a device records very high temperature in a furnace, the furnace needs to be immediately switched off, and this temperature data is useful only if actions are taken at that point in time. Enterprises need to understand the IoT solutions provided by IoT product vendors for real-time processing and analysis.

- Once IoT data is received, how will it be stored ensuring enough space for new information?

- How will inputs and outputs flow through devices without becoming clogged?

- For IoT use cases where device data need to be combined with non-device data (e.g., metadata about users and passwords), what solutions exist that can combine such disparate data to make the data meaningful?

Lessons Learned in Applying AI in IoT Use Cases (Applied IoT)

Artificial Intelligence is highly dependent on quality data to make right predictions. Once enterprises have the enough quality data, the way AI works is that a machine learning model is given a set of data. With this first set of data, the model performs computations and predicts an outcome. If the outcome is wrong, it readjusts the rule and applies the rule on the second set of data and predicts the outcome. This cycle goes on until the outcome is correct. Once the outcome is correct, data is fed multiple times again to determine the accuracy of the outcome. After applying the rule on thousands of data sets and consuming loads and loads of data, a model that does the right predictions is created. This is what machine learning is all about.

Applying AI in IoT use cases is not a very straightforward exercise and can lead into several challenges. Several times, Applied IoT can become a tedious and lengthy project if not planned well. There are four key lessons that I have personally learned in Applied IoT use cases, which are depicted in Figure 10-2.

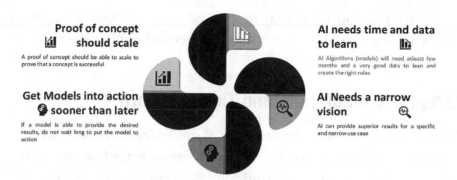

Proof of concept should scale
A proof of concept should be able to scale to prove that a concept is successful

AI needs time and data to learn
AI Algorithms (models) will need atleast few months and a very good data to lean and create the right rules

Get Models into action sooner than later
If a model is able to provide the desired results, do not wait long to put the model to action

AI Needs a narrow vision
AI can provide superior results for a specific and narrow use case

Figure 10-2. Applied IoT use case focus areas

POC Is Not Successful, Until It Can Scale

The first rule is that a concept cannot be treated as successful with a proof of concept. A concept is successful if a proof of concept is able to scale.

Let me explain this with a case study. One of the top luxury retail brands with 2000 plus retail stores in the United States wanted us to create an Artificial Intelligence utility using machine learning that is able to alert the store manager in less than five seconds if any celebrity turns up at their store. The store manager then will be able to greet the celebrity and give them a warm welcome to the store. We developed the Applied AI use case and deployed it at five stores in Alaska using 400 cameras, and it gave us encouraging results with more than 95% success rate. We implemented the POC using a facial recognition technique and machine learning patterns for around 5000 celebrities using millions of data sets. It worked great at Alaska.

We used the same technique in Michigan and other cities with 10,000 cameras, and the results were not encouraging. We missed 32% of the celebrities that entered the stores in both Michigan and Detroit since the data used was not sufficient to recognize all the celebrities around the region. This case study taught us that if a proof of concept proves that it works within five seconds with 400 cameras and 5000 celebrities, it does not mean it can work for 40,000 cameras and across 50,000 celebrities. So the first lesson learned is that a POC is not successful unless it is proven that it can scale.

AI Needs Enough Data and Time to Learn

To predict and provide accurate results, AI models require a lot of data and time. A medium to complex Applied AI use case needs at least six to nine months of learning time to provide 95% accuracy. A manufacturing customer called Seagate asked us to deploy several devices across their entire production line with the requirements to receive real-time insights on their product line failures, because traditionally if one of their units fails, the whole production line stops, which can cause several hundred of dollar losses. But the key ask from the customer was that we cannot tell them of these failures too early or too late; they needed to be informed just before any incident will occur. To achieve such near-real-time failure alerts, we needed to have an enormous amount of data, and the model needed several months of learning to predict the failures. After feeding millions of IoT data sets to the machine learning model for more than nine months, the model was able to predict failure just about 85% of the time.

Be Specific on What to Achieve

AI is very effective if it is given one specific narrow task to perform.

We were called to a hospital where there were high incidences of tuberculosis (TB) in a city. It was decided by the government to perform a TB test on each and every person from the city above 40 years of age. Though there were scans being performed on a mass scale across the city, the challenge hospitals faced is that after a chest X-ray is taken, it took two weeks for doctors to come back and confirm if a person is positive or negative to TB. For positive cases, in the two-week timeframe the risk was that the infected person would transmit the disease to others around them. AI was applied to solve this problem. We asked doctors to share all X-rays of patients and categorized them into two buckets, namely, TB positive and TB negative. TB positive are patients who were infected with TB, and the rest were categorized as TB negative. Machine learning models were run on thousands of X-rays which were pulled from the labs across the city. Models were trained over and over based on the positive and negative reports. After learning from millions of X-rays, finally the AI model was able to predict from an X-ray if a person is TB positive or negative in just one second. A 95% success rate was achieved by the algorithm.

So the key learning from this case study is that enterprises need to be very specific on what they want to achieve (predict) from AI. In the hospital case study, we used only X-rays as the means to predict tuberculosis in patients – we did not use MRI or CT scan.

Get a Model into Action If It Works Fine, Instead of Aspiring to Do More AI

If a model works fine, it is always recommended to put the model into action based on the use case.

We were in Copenhagen where I was shown a mobile app. The mobile app shows that in a proximity of 100 kilometers to my location how many food stores are there which has food items that will expire in the next two days. Using this data, stores provide discounts between 50% and 70% on the expiring food items. I found around 2000 food items within the 7-kilometer radius from my hotel, and once I clicked a specific store, it gave me a list of all expiring items in that store. I was also able to click a specific item, and the app gave me a list of all nearby stores where the expiring item was available. This is a simple app which did not require AI to perform the job, and a few simple rules were sufficient. The company that developed this app started with an aspiration to develop the app using AI algorithms, but soon they realized that the app does not need AI, and a few simple rules would be sufficient to extract the expiry date information from the food items and share it with users. This means that once you spend enough time collecting data and you see results, it is best to implement the rule instead of forcing yourself to do Applied AI.

The lesson learned with this example is that enterprises do not always need to force the data collected to do AI, even though they have been funded to do AI. If you can already do good with the data you have using predefined rules, please use the rules to achieve the business outcome.

Summary

In this chapter, we discussed the key differences between robotic process automation and Artificial Intelligence. We also discussed and understood the different subfields within Artificial Intelligence such as machine learning, deep learning, computer vision, natural language/speech processing, and cognitive computing that aim to build machines that can do things.

The importance of big data in Artificial Intelligence is clearly articulated in this chapter. Data science helps AIs figure out solutions to problems by linking similar data for future use. Fundamentally, data science allows AIs to find appropriate and meaningful information from those huge pools of data faster and more efficiently. It goes without saying that enterprises can be successful in applying Artificial Intelligence for IoT use cases only if they have quality data and are able to use the data in the right way.

Applying AI in IoT use cases is not a very straightforward exercise and can lead to several challenges if not planned well. We discussed about the four key learnings in an Applied IoT use case scenario:

1. IoT cannot be treated successful just because a POC has succeeded; POC should be able to scale, which is the first mantra.

2. The second mantra is to give enough data and time for AI models to learn.

3. The third mantra is to have a defined goal for AI
    models.

4. The fourth is to start using the AI models if they are
    giving results already instead of aspiring to do more AI.

It is essential for enterprises to ensure that they select the right Smart
IoT Gateways and IoT Cloud Platforms which have the support of Artificial
Intelligence. Secondly, IoT use cases need to be carefully chosen where AI
can play a role.

In the next chapter, we will discuss about the importance of data and
analytics in an IoT ecosystem, after which we will discuss about the big
data reference model.

PART IV

IoT Implementation Aspects

In this part, we will discuss about the execution aspects of IoT implementation, centered around big data and analytics, product organization, and the IoT product team.

CHAPTER 11

Big Data and Analytics

The early 1990s saw the rise of the information age. Network-connected computers and digital communication meant businesses were able to collect and leverage customer data to help develop new business models. This led to more efficient customer engagements, and the rise of online services has opened up a whole new way of working in many industries. Over the last 20 years, data strategy has become the foundation, and digital transformation is now largely reliant on data.

A digital transformation is not only about digitizing a channel or simply doing more things digitally, it has much broader scope than that. Digital transformation is about improving customer experiences and understanding the customers and competitors much better and using technology to address the business demands. On the other side, enterprises can also achieve efficiency in their operations with digital. To achieve these goals, enterprises need insights which purely come from data. This is one of the core reasons why data has become so much more important and hence why the "data-first" philosophy has become so popular. Data first effectively means that for any enterprise, data is the first thing to look at when making any business decisions.

Getting better data is key to eliminating the unknowns of a digital transformation. At Sprint, as Chief Data Officer Rob Roy explains, leaders call for "a new company culture that put data first."[1]

---

[1] www.mckinsey.com/business-functions/mckinsey-digital/our-insights/how-to-build-a-data-first-culture

© Venkatesh Upadrista 2021
V. Upadrista, *IoT Standards with Blockchain*,
https://doi.org/10.1007/978-1-4842-7271-8_11

Having a data-first mentality is a crucial first step; however, enterprises do need to put in place the processes and capabilities to be able to collect and make the data available in a fashion which can be used in the most timely and efficient way. The data also needs to be available at a speed by which businesses can make the right decisions and benefit from the insights generated from the data.

With the evolution of technology, data has evolved dramatically in recent years, in type, volume, and velocity. Earlier, we had landline phones, but now we have smartphones – they are making our lives as well as our phones smarter. Earlier, we were using floppies to store data, and now we use the cloud to store terabytes of data. Earlier, we used to talk over the phone, and now we send texts, pictures, and make video calls over WhatsApp. With technology advancement, we are generating a tremendous amount of data, and this is called big data. Big data is a term that describes the large volume of data ranging from structured, semistructured, and unstructured data.

Structured data is data which is organized into a formatted repository that is typically a database. It concerns all data which can be stored in a database in a table with rows and columns. It has relational keys and can easily be mapped into predesigned fields, for example, relational data.

Semistructured data is information that does not reside in a relational database but that has some properties that make it easier to analyze. With some process, one can store them in the relational database, for example, XML data.

Unstructured data is a data which is not organized in a predefined manner or does not have a predefined data model, for example, Word, PDF, text, media logs.

With big data, the deal is this data is not in a format that traditional database systems can handle. And apart from that, even the volume of data is also huge, which traditional database systems cannot handle. This has given rise to big data platforms which provide massive storage for any kind of data, enormous processing power, and the ability to handle virtually limitless concurrent tasks or jobs and any type of data (structured, semistructured, and unstructured). However, there are several challenges in a big data context, and the Big 4 Cs (Big 4 Challenges) are described as follows:

- Big data requires a large amount of storage space, and organizations must constantly scale their hardware and software in order to accommodate such increases. As these data sets grow exponentially with time, it gets extremely difficult to handle.

- The second is the velocity of data is high. What this means is that new data is being created at a very fast pace, and organizations need to have solutions to respond in real time.

- The third challenge is data variety. Data resides in a variety of different formats, such as text, images, video, and spreadsheets, and combining all this data to make sense of this data and prepare a report is a challenging task which needs to be addressed.

- The fourth key challenge that enterprises face with big data is security. Securing huge sets of data is one of the daunting challenges for big data platforms.

There are many matured solutions existing in the market to address the preceding challenges, but there is a need to carefully evaluate these solutions before bringing them into the enterprise.

Industrial revolution 4.0, also referred to as the fourth industrial revolution, is the term that we have been hearing since the last few years in an IoT context, and this term revolves around automation and AI within traditional manufacturing and industrial practices along with the whole technology innovation that is happening in the IT and OT industry. The fourth industrial revolution is becoming much broader across other industries as well and is transforming businesses by making machines smarter and a lot more talented, and all this is achieved with the massive data that is pumped in by these machines. With IoT at the helm of digital transformation, the complexity of managing data has increased several folds because until now we are talking about terabytes and petabytes of data, and with IoT we will be dealing with zettabytes of data. Size of IoT data has a major impact on all the Big 4 Cs, and therefore there is a need for a very elegant solution to handle and manage IoT data.

A megabyte (MB) is 1024 kilobytes. A gigabyte (GB) is 1024 megabytes, a terabyte (TB) is 1024 gigabytes, a petabyte is equal to 1000 terabytes, and 1 zettabyte is 1,000,000 petabytes, and so on. Just to give a view total of all US academic research libraries consume around 2 petabytes of storage.

Data management is an administrative process that includes acquiring, validating, storing, protecting, and processing required data to ensure the accessibility, reliability, and timeliness of the data for its users.

Data latency is the time it takes for data to travel from one place to another.

On one end of the spectrum, there are many enterprises that are coming up with platforms, tools, and solutions to implement IoT use cases, and on the other end enterprises are struggling to make sense of the enormous data coming from the devices, because of which these enterprises are unable to derive value from IoT use cases. The key point to address in IoT from a data context is to understand how to store such massive data, where to store this data (device, Smart IoT Gateway, or IoT Cloud Platform), how to process the data, and then how and when to analyze the data. Conceptually, this may look quite simple, but it is not so since there need to be very strong solutions to address each of these challenges very specific to IoT data, and not all traditional big data solutions suffice IoT data needs.

Figure 11-1 depicts the eight key capabilities that enterprises need to validate from a data perspective.[2] Based on the use cases, enterprises should decide where these capabilities need to exist, that is, at the Smart IoT Gateway or the IoT Cloud Platform, and accordingly products need to be purchased.

---

[2] Managing Your Outsourced IT Services Provider: How to Unleash the Full Potential of Your Global Workforce Paperback – 15 Dec. 2014 by Venkatesh Upadrista
Formula 4.0 for Digital Transformation, A Business-Driven Digital Transformation Framework for Industry 4.0 – May 27, 2021, by Venkatesh Upadrista

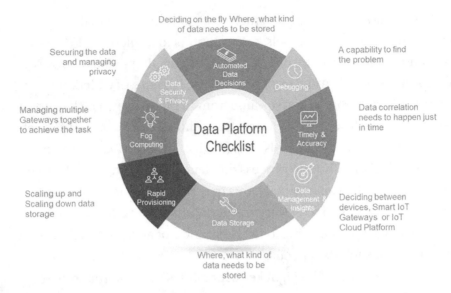

Figure 11-1. *Eight capabilities to validate while deciding a data platform*

Debugging Capabilities

There are a magnitude of devices that are connected in an IoT use case, and each of these devices sends enormous amounts of data. One of the pressing challenges in an IoT implementation is debugging. What this means is that if there is a problem (such as a performance issue in the IoT use case or a device malfunctioning to send right data) within the overall IoT architecture, there need to be strong solutions at either the IoT Gateway level or the IoT Cloud Platform level that can help debug the issue. The issue could be at the device level, at the network level, at the Smart IoT Gateway level, or at the IoT Platform level, and debugging where the problem is is extremely difficult. Enterprises need to look at vendors who have the right solutions to address this issue.

Timeliness and Accuracy of Data Brought Together

One of the most important aspects of IoT is that data needs to be timely and accurate. This means that related and relevant data from different devices and systems needs to come together at the same time which needs to be correlated in real time to make sense of the data. As an example, if we are reading a temperature data from a sensor related to the environment and if there is a failure in an equipment, it is essential that the exact time and the exact temperature data are correlated to derive a meaningful insight from the data. If we are unable to correlate these two data points, it is meaningless and there is no point in even collecting this data. This means that data from different devices needs to come with minimal to zero latency, else there is no value for this data later. Apart from timeliness and accuracy of the data, enterprises need to look at solutions that can bring both these data points together just in time to make sure that they are able to take some actions based on the insights generated from this data.

This brings to another important solution to be validated by enterprises before they choose any IoT Platform or Gateway – which vendor has the best solution that can bring together real-time data with precision and generate insights from the data just in time for timely actions.

Where Should Data Management and Insights Happen

The third area which enterprises need to focus on while embarking on their IoT journey is to determine where the complex process of data management happens. Once data is picked up from the sensors, it is ingested into the Smart IoT Gateways and in some cases is sent to the IoT Cloud Platform where data is cleansed and transformed, after which insights are generated from the data. Whether this needs to happen at the

Smart IoT Gateway level or the IoT Cloud Platform or on the devices needs to be answered based on which appropriate solutions need to be chosen. Such a decision depends on the use case and the industry for which use cases are being developed. As an example, in a smart agriculture use case, if a certain plant does not get enough water, we can come back the next day and water the plant. There is no major impact even if actions are taken at a later point in time or even if analytics goes wrong – in all such cases, economically it will still be all right to perform data management by the IoT Cloud Platform, where data latency will not cause major impact to the IoT use case. However, in use cases such as mining where we need to actually control the crude oil that comes out from the pipes, we need to be able to divert the crude oil at the right time to the right unit for processing, else there are massive losses that enterprises can incur. Furthermore, in a self-driving car use case, latency can lead to deaths or accidents. For all such time-critical use cases, it is important that data management and insights happen at the IoT Gateway level with a mandate that these Gateways will reside just near to the devices. In some cases, data management and insights need to be performed by the device itself.

Data Storage Considerations (What Data Needs to Be Stored and What Needs to Be Discarded

We discussed that IoT use cases generate a massive amount of data. However, it is important to understand that not all data generated by the devices are relevant for the enterprises, and this brings in a few important points that enterprises need to validate from a data perspective, which are listed as follows:

- What data needs to be stored

- What data needs to be discarded and when

- Which data needs to be retained for short-term purposes

- Which data needs to be retained for long-term purposes

All these need to be addressed from a data perspective before enterprises embark on their IoT use case development journey, else it will lead to failed IoT implementation. Hardware and storage specifications of Smart IoT Gateways or IoT Cloud Platforms are determined based on the storage requirements, data processing and data cleansing capability requirements, and computing and analytics capability. More specifically based on the short-term and long-term data storage needs, enterprises can determine the Smart IoT Gateway and IoT Cloud Platform required for their enterprise.

Rapid Provisioning of Storage Is Another Key Requirement

In the old days when data was collected from the satellites, we used to wait for the satellite to come over to our country. We had a very short window and bandwidth to collect the data, and during this period required data used to be collected to the extent possible, and then storage was made free for the next round of the satellite data collection. However, the agility required was not really to the level of minutes or microseconds. Today, IoT use cases have far higher demands on agility. Data is transmitted and needs to be collected at second levels or sometimes subsecond levels, and in many use cases, data would be relevant for that moment of time, such as temperature data. So enterprises need to be able to process the data as soon as they receive it, perform analytics and take actions, and then discard the data and keep storage free for the next set of data to come in. This brings in a key expectation from a data perspective in IoT use cases, which is the ability of the platforms to support rapid provisioning of storage. Enterprises need solutions that can scale up storage when required and scale down when the task is completed.

Data Management with Fog Computing

With the massive amount of data coming from each device in the IoT ecosystem, a single Smart IoT Gateway will not be able to handle the load especially for large-scale IoT use cases, such as in manufacturing or oil and gas industries. For all such use cases, there is a need to collect data from millions of devices and take actions just in time based on the insights generated from the data. A conglomerate of multiple IoT Gateways needs to be deployed to achieve the goals of the IoT use case. This is where fog computing comes into play. Fog computing or fog networking, also known as fogging, is an architecture that uses edge devices or IoT Gateways to carry out a substantial amount of computation, storage, and communication locally and routed over the Internet backbone

Enterprises need to look at data solutions that will address such a complex architecture where data and analytics need to be performed across multiple systems.

Automated Data Decisions

We discussed that enterprises need to determine what data needs to be stored, what data needs to be discarded, which data needs to be retained for short-term purposes, and which data needs to be retained for long-term purposes. Managing and storing all such data is currently manual, and there are very few solutions in the market that can perform this task automatically. To be more precise, enterprises need to look for automated solutions to perform the activity of storing and deleting the data either in Smart IoT Gateways or on IoT Cloud Platforms. Using Artificial Intelligence, this task can be performed, where machines can learn how enterprises had been managing their data in the past and predict how data needs to be managed in the future. There are companies that have started working on such solutions, but we are far from an elegant solution.

Data Security and Privacy Remains to Be a Big Concern Across Industries in IoT

It is quite important to understand the security solutions from a data perspective in an IoT context. Enterprises need to look at efficient solutions for encrypting the data in a way that nobody else can read data except the recipient. There need to be strong solutions for data protection, because a lot of data will be stored at the IoT Gateway or IoT Platform. Enterprises need to look at solutions that address how data is purged, and that purged data cannot be recovered again because enterprise data is always very sensitive. Another area in a similar context is the data privacy. From a data perspective, enterprises need to look at solutions where the data of one user of a department is not accessible to others.

(Big) Data-First Reference Model

The key to success for any organization is how well big data is being used in the organization to make business decisions. To make the right decisions, enterprises need to get the correct and relevant data at the right time to the business. This is one of the reasons why the "data first" terminology has become so prominent. The strategy of data first is how we enable enterprises to move toward a data-driven organization where each and every major business decision is made from insights received from data. To make a data-first strategy come true, data journeys need to be smartly managed. With IoT, a data-first strategy is a mandate since IoT use cases use data as the primary vehicle to succeed.

Though enterprises understand the importance of data and have tried to embark on a data journey, many of them have seen failed results. Without a fully implemented data platform and a standard architecture, organizations cannot expect to have sound data hygiene practices in place that will help them to be successful. Figure 11-2 provides an overview on the data-first reference model, using which enterprises can define a standard operating model that can help them succeed in their data journey for IoT use cases.

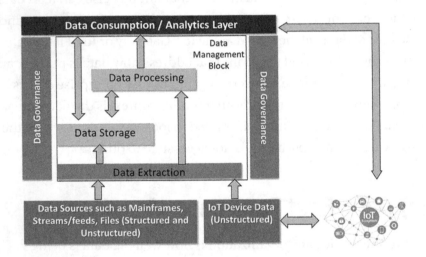

Figure 11-2. *Data-first reference architecture*

The first block is the data source, where data from external and internal sources arrive at the enterprise. In the IoT ecosystem, IoT data will arrive from devices, and other sets of data will come from sources such as external streams, feeds, mainframe systems, digital twins, or simple Excel files. This data is sometimes directly stored in the data lake or is processed and then stored in the date lake.

The second block is where data storage and data processing happen. This is where data is acquired (data extraction layer) and then cleaned and refined to make it usable. This data is then made available for consumption in the appropriate format. Data management is a process that includes acquiring, validating, storing, and processing data to ensure the accessibility, reliability, and timeliness of the data for its users.

The third block is data governance, which is the process of managing the availability, usability, integrity, and security of the data in enterprise systems, based on internal data standards and policies that also control data usage.

The fourth block is called the consumption layer where data is consumed by different parties such as analytics platforms, reporting tools, or directly by data scientists or business users.

The Data Source

A data source is simply the point where data enters the organization. It can be structured data which comprises clearly defined data types whose pattern makes them easily searchable, or unstructured data which is "everything else" and comprises data that is usually not as easily searchable, including formats like audio, video, and social media postings, or semistructured data. As part of the IoT ecosystem apart from data from regular sources, there are a lot of machine data that are sent by devices, which are called passive, active, or dynamic data.

Passive data is sent by devices which have sensors that do not actively communicate. These are sensors that must be activated before they can transmit data, and they only produce data when asked to do so. For example, a sensor that measures groundwater saturation only produces current data when the API is invoked. In a passive data collection, since the sensors need to be managed, the application must take on the logic needed to do so. These are typically sensors that are low power and exist in remote locations.

Active data (also called streaming data) means that sensors are continuously streaming data such as from connected cars or temperature sensors. Unlike passive data, these sensors constantly send the data at predefined intervals. For all such kind of devices, it is essential that IoT Gateways are able to absorb the data in near real time, and the applications need sophisticated IoT data communications capabilities. Data cannot be lost, it must be correctly parsed from the stream just in time and placed in the correct format for storage and processing so that actions can be taken based on the insights generated.

Ddynamic data is the most sophisticated data that is sent by devices (sensors) that communicate dynamically (bidirectional) with IoT applications, such as a smart thermostat. These types of devices carry out a conversation with IoT applications. This allows a full range of capabilities, including the ability to change the data that is produced, change the format of the data, change the frequency, and even deal with security issues and provide automated software updates to dynamically deal with issues.

Most of the new IoT devices that are being manufactured these days for IoT use cases are built for dynamic data.

In an enterprise-level IoT implementation, we all will be dealing with all the three types of IoT data – passive, active, and dynamic – in any of our current IoT use cases.

The data management block is where the data arrives at the enterprise from data sources. One of the first steps in setting up a data strategy is assessing what enterprises have in the data source and whether the IoT Gateway has the capability to retrieve data from all types of devices and other sources across all three types of data (i.e., active, passive, and dynamic).

The Data Storage Layer

The data storage layer is where enterprise data lives once it is gathered from different sources and devices. It receives data from the various data sources and stores it in the most appropriate manner that is specific to the organization needs. Based on the use cases, in some instances data from sources are directly stored in the storage (called raw data), and in other cases data are transformed and then stored in the data storage (called gold data).

As depicted in Figure 11-1, the data storage layer sits at the bottom of the reference model. These are the technologies that store masses of raw data which come from traditional sources, such as online transaction processing (OLTP) databases, and less structured sources, such as log files, sensors, web analytics, documents, and media archives.

Increasingly, storage is taking place in the cloud or on virtualized local resources. Organizations are moving away from legacy storage toward commoditized hardware and more recently to managed services offered by the likes of Amazon, such as Amazon S3.

As the volume of data generated and stored by companies has started to explode, sophisticated but accessible systems and tools are being developed.

Data Extraction Layer and Data Processing Layer

Data extraction is the process of bringing in relevant data that has been created by a source outside the organization. IoT data, especially streaming data coming from IoT devices, cannot be handled by traditional data extraction solutions, and enterprises need to look at solutions that can effectively extract active, passive, and dynamic IoT data. As an example, Microsoft Azure has Stream Analytics that can perform extraction of IoT data.

Data processing is the process of cleaning and refining the data for enterprise use. For any type of data, when it enters an organization (in most cases, there are multiple data sources), it is most likely either not clean or not in the format that can be reported or analyzed directly by users inside or outside of the organization. Data processing is therefore needed first, which usually includes data cleansing, standardization, transformation, and aggregation. Apache Spark, PostgreSQL, and Amazon Redshift are good examples of tools which can carry out this job.

Data Consumption Layer

This layer consumes the output provided by the data processing layer. Enterprises can run queries to answer questions the business is asking, slice and dice the data, build dashboards, and create visualizations, using one of many advanced tools. In some cases, data in this layer is directly consumed by users within the organization and by entities external to the organization, such as customers, vendors, partners, and suppliers.

In IoT use cases, actions are taken based on the insights generated in the data consumption layer. As an example, if the temperature of a specific machinery goes beyond a certain range, tools within the consumption layer detect such an event in real time, and they send a command to the IoT device to shut down the machine.

IoT Use cases requires time-based analytics to be performed first at the per-device level and then aggregated into overall numbers to provide a view on the overall state of the cluster of devices. This is a complex case of aggregation across the device estate that needs to be rolled up. As an example, in some instances a single temperature data can trigger an action, and in some use cases, an average temperature over time becomes crucial to perform a task. There are several analytic tools available in the market such as AWS IoT Analytics and AWS IoT SiteWise that can perform specific actions based on IoT data.

Data Governance

Data governance (DG) is the process of managing the availability, usability, integrity, and security of the data in enterprise systems, based on internal data standards and policies that also control data usage. Effective DG ensures that data is consistent and trustworthy and does not get misused. It is increasingly critical as organizations face new data privacy regulations and rely more and more on data analytics to help optimize operations and drive business decision-making.

Data stewardship is a functional role in data management and governance, with the responsibility of ensuring that data policies and standards are implemented and followed within the enterprise.

Data integrity is the maintenance of, and the assurance of, data accuracy and consistency over its entire life cycle and is a critical aspect to the design, implementation, and usage of any system that stores, processes, or retrieves data.

A well-designed DG program typically includes a governance team, a steering committee that acts as the governing body, and a group of data stewards. They work together to create the standards and policies for governing data as well as implementation and enforcement procedures that are primarily carried out by the data stewards. The big data setup and governance should be performed at the enterprise level rather than in business unit silos – this is mandatory for enterprises to succeed.

While data governance is a core component of an overall data management strategy, organizations should focus on the desired business outcomes of a governance program instead of the data itself. Without effective DG, data inconsistencies in different systems across an organization might not be resolved. For example, customer names may be listed differently in sales, logistics, and customer service systems. This could complicate data integration efforts and create data integrity issues that affect the accuracy of enterprise reporting and analytics applications. In addition, data errors might not be identified and fixed, further affecting analytics accuracy.

Poor DG can also hamper regulatory compliance initiatives, which could cause problems for companies that need to comply with new data privacy and protection laws, such as the European Union's General Data Protection Regulation (GDPR) and the California Consumer Privacy Act (CCPA). An enterprise DG program typically results in the development of common data definitions and standard data formats that are applied in all business systems, boosting data consistency for both business and compliance uses.

A key goal of DG is to break down data silos in an organization. Such silos commonly build up when individual business units deploy separate systems without centralized coordination or an enterprise data architecture. DG aims to harmonize the data in those systems through a collaborative process, with stakeholders from the various business units participating.

Another DG goal is to ensure that data is used properly, both to avoid introducing data errors into systems and to block potential misuse of personal data about customers as well as other sensitive information. This can be accomplished by creating uniform policies on the use of data, along with procedures to monitor usage and enforce the policies on an ongoing basis. In addition, DG can help to strike a balance between data collection practices and privacy mandates.

Besides more accurate analytics and stronger regulatory compliance, the benefits that DG provides include improved data quality, lower data management costs, and increased access to needed data for data scientists, analysts, and business users.

Ultimately, DG can help improve business decision-making by giving executives better information.

Summary

In this chapter we have discussed about the data-first mindset, which is one of the most important elements for enterprises to be successful using IoT. Enterprises need to put in place the processes and capabilities to be able to collect and make the data available in a way that it can be used in the most timely and efficient manner by IoT use cases. The data also needs to be available at a speed that will enable businesses to make the right decisions and benefit from the insights generated from the data.

We also discussed that the key area to address in IoT from the data context is to define solutions around how to store large data sets, where to store this data (device, Smart IoT Gateway, or IoT Cloud Platform), how to process the data, and then how and when to analyze the data.

We discussed about the eight key capabilities that enterprises need to validate from the data perspective, which are listed in the following. Based on the use cases, enterprises should decide where these capabilities need to exist, that is, at the Smart IoT Gateway or the IoT Cloud Platform, and accordingly products need to be purchased.

1. Debugging capabilities of the platform

2. Timeliness and accuracy of data coming from the devices

3. Deciding on where data management and analytics need to happen

4. Data storage considerations

5. Rapid provisioning of data

6. Fog computing capabilities

7. Automated data decision capabilities (what data to store or discard for the short and the long term)

8. Data security solutions

Finally, in the last section we discussed about the data-first reference model, which constitutes of four blocks. The first block is the data source, where data from external and internal sources arrives at the enterprise. The second block is where data storage and data processing happen. This is where data is acquired (data extraction layer) and then cleaned and refined to make it usable. The third block is data governance, which is the process of managing the availability, usability, integrity, and security of the data in enterprise systems; and the fourth block is called the consumption layer, where data is consumed by different parties, such as analytics platforms, reporting tools, or directly by data scientists or business users.

Moving from a project-based to a product-based organization is essential for enterprises to succeed with IoT, which we will discuss in the next chapter. We will discuss about transforming to a product organization for IoT use case implementation and associated benefits.

CHAPTER 12

Product Mindset for IoT Use Case Implementation

Digital transformation can mean different things to different enterprises. For some enterprises, digital transformation is adopting technologies such as AI, RPA, or big data. For other organizations, digital transformation is the use of new age technologies over traditional ones to build a scalable IT environment. One final interpretation is that digital transformation means achieving the desired speed at which an organization can bring new features to the market.

All the preceding definitions are correct in the respective context; however, digital transformation is all about achieving speed, agility, reliability, and cost-effectiveness in whole rather than in parts to achieve a business outcome. With IoT, all these benefits are achieved in much faster and superior pace, and therefore IoT has become one of the most widely experimented digital transformation initiatives for enterprises.

In this chapter, we are going to discuss about the importance of product-centric enterprises as opposed to project-centric enterprises and the reasons why product-centric operating model is a must for enterprises embarking on their IoT journey.

© Venkatesh Upadrista 2021
V. Upadrista, *IoT Standards with Blockchain*,
https://doi.org/10.1007/978-1-4842-7271-8_12

What is a project or a project organization?

In simple terms, a project is a container for all the activities that are laid out in sequence. We plan and then we analyze, we design, we implement, and then we test everything. And at the end, we ship everything that works well. A project has three main interdependent constraints, namely, time, cost, and scope. This is also known as the project management triangle as depicted in Figure 12-1.

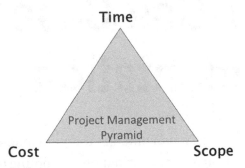

Figure 12-1. *Project management pyramid*

This means to deliver a project, a fixed scope is required, after which the fixed cost and time are decided. As a good project manager, you deliver your project on time, scope, and budget.

A typical project runs between six months and a few years. A project-based approach works well if the baseline (e.g., requirements) for the project does not change during the course of project execution. In an IoT context, the baselines are ever changing – as an example, there may be 100 devices to connect today, and we would have 10,000 tomorrow. This is one of the reasons why organizations following a project model for IoT use cases are failing even though they are delivering on cost, time, and scope. A scope cannot be fixed in an IoT context for longer durations.

Not only in an IoT context but project-based approaches have proven to fail even in a normal software development engagement. A quote of the former CEO of a large phone manufacturer named ABC Mobile, who lost their business to their competitor (Apple), comes to my mind during this discussion. He said that he did not do anything wrong, but somehow he lost. The projects his company was performing were all running fine, they embraced the Agile methodology, and they had an awesome track record of really building phone after phone. But while ABC Mobile was building phones in a project approach, the market changed, and people were not buying the kind of phones which this company was selling, and they lost their complete user base to another company (Apple).

This is the biggest challenge with project-based organizations. A project manager comes up with the plan for the scope, schedule, and the budget which gets approved by a steering board, and then a couple of weeks later, this project is initiated, and then it is executed with the only goal to deliver the project based on the scope, ignoring the market, and by the time the project is delivered, the market changes.

The above is one perspective on ABC Mobile. In contrast to the preceding discussion, another interesting perspective about ABC Mobile is that they realized a year before that something is going to change fundamentally with phones. They knew that there was going to be phones with large glass screens, and Apple was going to make something called an iPhone. With that, ABC Mobile realized that customer experience with the mobile phones was going to be basically driven by software (with widgets and app stores), and it will no longer going to be physical buttons.

A lot of people think that ABC Mobile missed the revolution by not realizing that they needed big glass screens. However, the reality is that they knew a year before that the industry will move toward software-driven phones. Once they realized it, they brought in some of the best consultants, they hired more developers, and they realized that they needed to become software innovators and develop in a more iterative manner – and they did this all. They embraced the Agile methodology to develop phones. In 2009, I remember ABC Mobile was the poster child to adopt the Agile methodology, their employees were trained in Agile, and everyone started developing using the Agile methodology. The main focus for ABC Mobile during that time was on agile trainings and embracing the Agile methodology. This is what ABC Mobile called the transformation.

Within the company, developers were trained on Agile, they were using agile tools, using agile methods, and building the phones, but nothing was moving faster. The CEO was measuring the transformation through these metrics, whether people were trained on Agile and whether they were using the agile toolkits, and with these metrics it appeared to the executive that the whole transformation was on track.

But then this way of working was actually not solving their core problem. The core problem ABC Mobile had was with their software architecture. The operating system they had did not allow them to fit the big screens effectively or support an app store. By the time they realized this gap, iPhone was released, and ABC Mobile went out of the market. ABC Mobile adopted a project-based structure, though they adopted Agile which was the main reason for this failure. They operated in a project-based structure with a fixed scope, time, and cost (using Agile), and this turned out to be quite disconnected in terms of how they were measuring their agility and how value is actually flowing in the organization.

From the preceding discussion, it is very clear that technology or processes cannot solve business problems. Understanding the market and adapting to changes are the mantras for any business to be successful, and these cannot be achieved in a project-based structure.

Product Organization

A product organization is all about delivering business outcomes or business value in shorter intervals, keeping in mind the market changes or changes within the enterprise and adapting immediately to these changes. Forrester defines an outcome as an achieved end state that can be verified through measurable results.[1] An outcome could be additional revenues, higher customer satisfaction, new customer acquisition, and so on.

---

[1] https://go.forrester.com/blogs/10-04-26-how_would_you_define_ customer_outcome/

An example of an outcome is listed as follows:

By July 2022, we aim to increase the sales of clothing by 25% by making the checkout process faster and more transparent for shoppers who are frustrated with the time it takes to purchase our product.

Once we define an outcome we want to achieve, it probably may be too much to do in a short timeframe, so we have to really ask what is the highest possible value and what is the minimum viable product that can be shipped in shortest possible time so that it can be released to the market to validate the acceptance of the feature or product.

An example of the highest possible value and minimum viable product outcome is listed as follows:

In the next three months, we aim to increase the sales of kids clothing by 60% by adding a quick checkout option available to shoppers. This can be enabled by installing IoT devices to kiosk and supporting with contactless options.

Many enterprises are still operating in project mode. Transforming from a project to a product (outcome based) thinking organization is the need for any enterprise to be successful.

It is very easy to talk about business outcomes and transforming from a project to a product organization. But the ground realities are very different, especially for many enterprises that are in business from the last several decades.

When we talk about making the change from a project to a product, there are four impediments that every enterprise is challenged with:

- IT is disconnected from business and vision – This means that having IT and OT to work with business is the biggest hurdle with almost all enterprises.

- Executives are tracking activities and not business results – This is clearly driven by the fact that the success of an IT manager in an enterprise is determined by how many tasks are completed as against the plan.

- Project funding is broken – This is one of the major issues especially with large enterprises. Projects are still funded on an annual funding cycle, which usually are for a 12–18-month cycle.

- The business feels IT is solving its own problems – This is because of the fact that IT is generally focused on making developers more productive, reducing defects, ensuring business continuity is maintained, and so on, none of which delivers business outcomes.

Most of the enterprises these days want to switch from linear-based projects to more products and product developments. When I speak about product organization, I remember a CIO asking me on how unicorns such as Google, Amazon, and Microsoft do long-term planning despite being so big. The answer is that these companies never do long-term planning, and their budget cycles are three to six months. What this means is that the board comes together every three to six months to allocate budgets based on the market needs, and they operate with a product-centric mindset.

It is really hard to respond to any changing market or internal enterprise needs with a lengthy budgeting cycle such as 12 months or 18 months. And if anyone has to do and achieve success with such a lengthy cycle, they need to have an absolute forecasting ability to determine what they need to do for the next 18 months, and this is an ability no one possesses. Therefore, enterprises are bound to be disappointed with the results.

With a product organization, there is a hypothesis that enterprises fund; the hypothesis is converted to a prototype, it is tested in the market, and once the market responds positively, further enhancements are done, and functionalities are released to the market in very short intervals. This concept is called "Hypothesis to Cash." We are going to discuss about Hypothesis to Cash in the subsequent sections and its importance for IoT use cases. To make the concept of Hypothesis to Cash a reality, business and IT need to work together and should share a common goal of business outcomes. IT needs to start conversations with business about business outcomes and align technology solutions to those business outcomes. Enterprises need to move away from a contractual relationship between business and IT to a one team model. A one team model is where IT and business have the same targets – this is what a product organization is all about.

Such a transformation cannot be achieved in one or two weeks or one to two months; it takes time and there should be acceptance from both IT and business teams on the model. Business takes the lead in a product organization model, and the IT team works with business to realize the business outcomes. From the technology perspective, the IT team brings in methodologies to deliver faster results. In an IoT context, the IT team is referred to as a team with IT and OT together, also called an IoT team.

A product in IoT terms is an IoT use case. Like a normal product organization, IoT product organization also has a measurable outcome, offers quicker business results, improved customer experiences, improved efficiency, reduced friction within the organization, and more flexibility. All of this results in increased trust across the business since an IoT use case has its own measurable business benefit. A product-centric setup allows for better engagement and full ownership between IoT team and business units since product owners from the business side are part of the team delivering the IoT use case end to end. The measurable outcome in a product-based organization for every enhancement or new business functionality is based on how fast the new functionality is released to the market, how many new customers a new feature is able to attract, and if the customer satisfaction has improved after adding a new feature to the overall product. Alternatively, if an IoT use case is developed to increase operation efficiency, outcomes are measured as how much gain the product has brought to the business, such as reducing machine downtimes or increasing utilization of machineries in a manufacturing context or automatic detection of diseases with accuracy in a healthcare context. This measurement contrasts with traditional metrics in a project organization where for every new business functionality development, teams are measured on the number of defects in production, quality of the resources, and so on. Traditional metrics in product organizations do not vanish but are treated as secondary measures to the product success.

IoT Product Life Cycle with Product Mindset

So far, we discussed about product organization. In an IoT world, enterprises will not be developing products, they will be developing IoT use cases. It is essential to think about IoT use case development with a product mindset rather than a project mindset. What this means is that the product life cycle needs to be followed for IoT use case development, and all principles of product development need to be applied. A product mindset means that IoT use cases are developed as similar to any new products. In an IoT world, products are replaced with IoT use cases.

An IoT use case life cycle constitutes of five phases as similar to the product life cycle: introduction, growth, maturity, decline, and stabilization. This is depicted in Figure 12-2.

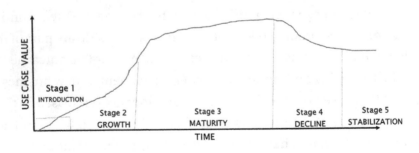

Figure 12-2. *IoT use case life cycle*

- The first phase is the introduction phase. During this phase, an IoT use case is launched with minimal features. This is where IoT proofs of concepts are developed. The IoT use case is put into live, and users are encouraged to start measuring the benefits from the use case.

- After a period of time, the IoT use case starts demonstrating measurable benefits to the enterprise business, and then the use case enters the growth phase where new features are added. During the growth phase, users are delighted with more enriched functionalities that make the IoT use case more and more attractive. Depending on the use cases, IoT can either increase revenue for the enterprise or improve efficiency of the enterprise, such as making the manufacturing equipment reduce downtime or enable predictive maintenance for the equipment.

- In the maturity phase, new features that can bring value to the enterprise are added, but each feature is validated thoroughly from the benefit perspective. This is because, in this phase, sales or efficiency remains fairly constant, and therefore for every new feature that is added to the use case, there need to be measurable benefits.

- After a while, the IoT use case becomes business as usual. No additional features to the use case can bring further value to the enterprise. This is the decline phase where the IoT use case product team is ramped down to the bare minimum.

- The final stage is the stabilize phase where development is frozen for the use case, and only the operations team remains for the specific use case. The operations team manages the day-to-day operations of the use case, and any new enhancements to the use case are thoroughly validated from a cost-benefit perspective before being undertaken by the team.

Hypothesis to Cash

Introduction, growth, and maturity are the three phases where most IoT use case development and enhancement happens, and this is where the Hypothesis to Cash model is applied for each new feature that is added to a use case.

The Hypothesis to Cash model has four phases as depicted in Figure 12-3. It is mandatory that business, IT, and OT teams work together in all phases of the IoT use case development.

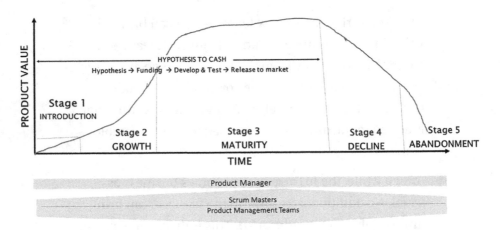

Figure 12-3. *Hypothesis to Cash*

Hypothesis – This is a phase in which a new idea of a use case or an enhancement is brainstormed. A hypothesis in an IoT product organization is an idea (or more precisely a use case) that is proposed so that it can be tested to validate if it has a potential to generate value for the enterprise.

Funding – This is a phase in which funding is approved based on the acceptance of the hypothesis.

Develop and test – Once funding is approved, the idea is converted into a prototype (proof of concept). A prototype is an early sample, model, or release of an IoT use case built to test the hypothesis. The IoT use case needs to be built with reasonable functionality so that benefits can be validated.

Release to the production (and generate value) – Once developed, the prototype is released into production to validate acceptance of the idea from users and associated benefits. Based on the benefits delivered, Hypothesis to Cash is applied to enhance the feature with full functionality.

As you can see, an IoT use case has its own life cycle, and, with product thinking, an enterprise business can be broken down into multiple IoT use cases. A cumulation of all these use cases forms the enterprise operating model.

Agile Software Development Methodology in IoT Use Case Development

Project and product management has existed for decades, as have many different software development life cycle models. Over time, people developed what have become today's standards, which are treated as the guiding principles in the IT industry. In the modern world, technical challenges and customer requirements have revolutionized the need for better life cycle models to keep pace with changing demands. Modern practices and principles differ from those of the past.

Traditional software methodologies have lost their appeal almost a decade back due to limitations in their ability to accommodate changing needs and to control large, complex projects.

Anyone who has been in the industry for a while and worked on a large development project has probably experienced the "big design up front" (BDUF) approach to software development, which is highly risky because it does not support change. Most people are unable to describe exactly how the entire system should behave up front. More often than not, the business thinks they have got it right at first, but begin to change their minds as more analysis is performed and they get closer to the details. While traditional methodologies have worked for some organizations in the past, and may still work in some circumstances, for many organizations they only add to the frustration caused by unmanageable changing requirements, ultimately leading to unpredictable project outcomes.

The current and rapidly changing environment imposes constraints on quality, time, and costs, as well as legal, cultural, and logical parameters. In addition, several principles are being modernized to keep pace with the industry. Agile is one such methodology which has moved from the so-called "emerging methodology" to the mainstream "development methodology," especially in product developments. This is providing value to the customer by providing better transparency, better requirements trade-offs, faster time to market, reduced defects, and enabling the building of a mature, quality product.

Agile is a software development methodology in which systems are built in increments, where requirements and solutions evolve through a collaboration between cross-functional teams and over a period of time. Agile methods generally promote a lightweight product management process that includes frequent monitoring and adapting to changes quickly that encourages teamwork, self-organizing, and self-accountability. In addition, there is a set of good practices that allows for rapid delivery of high-quality products, as well as a business approach that aligns development with business needs and the organization's goals. Scrum is one such Agile methodology where software is built in smaller increments called sprints. A sprint is a short, timeboxed period when a scrum team works to complete a set amount of work. Sprints are at the very heart of Scrum and Agile methodologies. A combination of multiple sprints is called a release.

Agile – A De Facto Methodology for IoT Use Case Development

IoT is all about developing use cases for future in the nimblest fashion that can revolutionize the way business is conducted; future-proofing enterprises for the continuously changing internal factors, external competitors, industry trends, and new technologies; and finally reducing costs.

With this in mind, following an agile approach to rolling out new IoT use cases for an enterprise is mandatory.

Figure 12-4 depicts the benefits of Agile methodology, thereby implying that Agile is the best way to go for any digitally transformed enterprise.

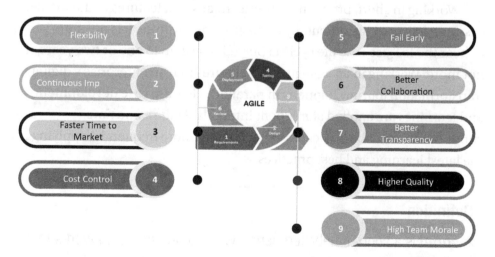

Figure 12-4. Benefits of Agile

Flexibility

At the heart of Agile is the flexibility it offers in developing features of IoT use cases in iterations and deploying to production or production-like infrastructure.

Traditionally, new business initiatives are carved out with detailed requirements and little room for change, particularly as the project kicks off. The agile process accepts change and even expects it. If the team discovers that a different solution provides better results for their specific challenges, then they have the flexibility to switch. Likewise, if the business priorities change halfway, changes can be adopted much faster with Agile.

Continuous Learning and Developments

Agile teams are always learning, collaborating, and adjusting throughout regular iterations, reviewing what is working well and what can be improved. It means everyone has the time to not only expand their own knowledge, but all learnings can be identified, shared, and applied to the IoT use case development at each stage before moving forward.

Frequent Value Delivered

Working in short, productive sprints means that features of the IoT use case are delivered incrementally as the use case evolves. It is not surprising to hear the IoT use case life cycle expected to last up to one or two years, if not more. Working in an agile manner ensures that an enterprise's digital transformation journey happens in parallel to IoT use case development, and learnings are applied at frequent intervals. At the same time, continuously valuable use cases are delivered, more frequently, applying the latest learning and best practices.

Definition

A *sprint* is a short, timeboxed period when a product team works to complete a set amount of work.

Cost Control

Keeping sprint lengths the same throughout the IoT use case development allows the team to know exactly how much work can be accomplished and therefore the cost for each sprint. It also allows for budget refinements on a regular basis and changes to be made, often without exorbitant costs as a result.

Failing Early or No Failure

An agile approach to IoT use case development practically eliminates the chance of failing late in the process, which means there are no failures to a program as a whole. Daily updates, constant communication, regular testing, and collaborative feedback along with working use cases at the end of each sprint ensure nothing is missed and every issue is captured and dealt with early.

Higher Collaboration, Communications, and Engagement

IoT use cases will never be achieved with just one team. To be successful, the OT team, business, and IT units need to work in unison with a clear vision of the organizational challenges that need to be solved. Agile in a product enterprise encourages regular communication, constant collaboration, feedback sessions, and continuous stakeholder management, which are critical to the success of any product team.

Full Transparency

Regular collaboration, communication, and updates between multiple agile teams yield higher visibility across the business. With working use cases being delivered in shorter intervals, this transparency and visibility on the progress of IoT use case development becomes much more apparent. Agile ensures every team member up to the key stakeholders have the opportunity to know how the use case development is going. Daily updates and progress charts offer concrete, tangible ways to track progress and manage expectations at every level.

High Quality

The quality of work improves within an agile environment because testing and optimization starts from the very beginning. It naturally allows for the early sight of any issues and relevant adjustments to be made quickly. Agile in an IoT perspective also encourages teams to embrace innovation and technological excellence.

Higher Team Morale

There is no change or innovation without people. To create a highly motivated and high-performing IoT use case development team requires a level of self-management, the encouragement of creativity, time to reflect, regular knowledge sharing, and continuous learning – all of which are advantages of the agile process. Teams that are constantly working overtime to meet unrealistic deadlines will inevitably lack the inclination, or time, to think about anything else other than the task at hand, stifling the creation of any new and innovative ideas.

Summary

In this chapter, we discussed about the challenges enterprises face with a project organization and the importance of transforming to a product-centric organization. We discussed that a product organization is all about delivering business outcomes or business value in shorter intervals, keeping in mind the market changes or changes within the enterprise and adapting immediately to these changes. In an IoT world, it is essential to think about IoT use case development with a product mindset rather than a project mindset.

Subsequently, we discussed the five phases of an IoT use case life cycle which constitutes of introduction, growth, maturity, decline, and abandonment. Introduction, growth, and maturity are the three phases where most IoT use case development and enhancement happens, and this is where the Hypothesis to Cash model is applied for each new feature that is added to a use case. The Hypothesis to Cash model has four phases, namely, the hypothesis (new idea generation), funding (idea funding), development and test, and finally production release.

Finally, we discussed about the Agile software development methodology and the benefits it brings to enterprises. Agile is a software development methodology in which systems are built in increments, where requirements and solutions evolve through a collaboration between cross-functional teams and over a period of time.

In the next chapter, we will discuss about how an IoT product team needs to be created for enterprises to be successful and achieve the desired benefits from IoT.

CHAPTER 13

IoT Product Team

Traditionally, OT teams are instrumental in maintaining and scaling lean factory operations. They ensure that all control and automation technologies enable seamless production and operation processes. OT has been intentionally separated from IT, and they have different people, goals, policies, and projects. This independence drives OT teams to be agile and efficient on the shop floor. In recent years, IT-OT integration has taken several industries by storm and represents a new source of data that can be leveraged to increase factory efficiency using IT. This new era of connectivity presents the OT team with many opportunities to further manage, automate, and optimize the shop floor and production processes. Unfortunately, without IT and OT team integration, these opportunities cannot be capitalized upon in IoT use cases. Consider this: if shop floor data is not integrated with data from IT systems, operational excellence and production optimization are difficult to achieve since gaps in the current business process cannot be easily determined.

This brings in a new perspective in terms of the operating model for IoT which is to integrate IT and OT teams to make IoT aspiration a success for enterprises. As we discussed earlier, security is one of the major concerns in IoT, but this cannot stop an enterprise toward the integration. Enterprises need to find out ways to improve security postures both from IT and OT perspectives and move ahead with their IoT journey.

On the other side, there is an enormous amount of data that is pumped from the OT devices, and traditional data management systems simply cannot handle such a load. It is impossible to use traditional IT systems for

© Venkatesh Upadrista 2021
V. Upadrista, *IoT Standards with Blockchain*,
https://doi.org/10.1007/978-1-4842-7271-8_13

real-time decision-making with such huge and disparate sets of data. With IoT, enterprises will have interconnected machines, and these machines generate a lot of data that needs to be analyzed in real time to give a full picture of what is happening on the floor or even in a single machine. For example, in a shoe manufacturing plant, the machine creating soles can notify the team responsible for sole stitching when there is an unexpected delay or backlog, allowing them to switch to other tasks while maintenance is carried out. This facility-wide visibility is simply impossible without data connectivity, and as such having a big data platform is a must for enterprises embarking on an IoT journey. As we discussed in Chapter 11, with a big data platform enterprises will be able to bring in all kinds of data from the operational equipment and create a centralized IoT network. Subsequently, this network can be connected with the existing IT to generate insights.

IoT Product Team

Based on the preceding discussion, the key roles that are required to make an IoT successful are listed in Figure 13-1.

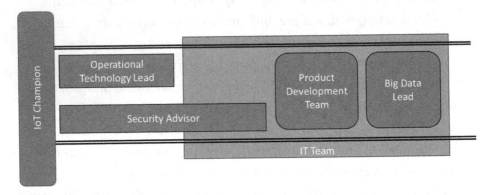

Figure 13-1. *IoT product team*

Operational Technology Lead

The OT lead brings in the shop floor expertise and has complete understanding of the machineries and production processes used within the shop floor for the specific use case that is identified for implementation. To integrate an OT system into the IT world, one needs to understand the ins and outs of things IT has typically not considered, such as

- Automation technologies used on the shop floor

- Environmental factors (temperatures, chemical exposure, etc.)

- Real-time intelligence systems

- Redundancy protocols

- Regulatory requirements

- Shop floor setup and infrastructure

An enterprise can only embark on IoT product development if the team planning and performing the integration understands how operations and business issues work and discovers ways that IT can help OT to deploy new technology to improve operations. This is one of the main reasons why an OT lead is required in the team. An OT lead forms part of the core team in an IoT journey.

Security Advisor

Security in IoT is of paramount importance. Decades ago, when corporations first started leveraging client/server networks and the Internet, they did not think about security until criminals realized they could hack into IT systems to manipulate them and steal money and data. OT environments today face similar challenges when connecting industrial control system (ICS) technologies to the Internet. Until recently, OT was interconnected with proprietary, vendor-based closed connections and protocols that could not be accessed remotely. Now that ICS technologies are moving toward exposing themselves to the Internet, IT security challenges have become part of OT environments. This is one of the reasons why security considerations should be planned from day one in IoT, and a security advisor is the one who plays this role.

Any OT system that needs to be integrated with IT systems needs to be analyzed thoroughly from a cyber security perspective. Security in the context of IoT means how IT systems will interact with the devices that are part of the OT systems and the security pertaining to these systems, sensors, and devices. Choosing devices that have built-in security features, and shortlisting capable IoT device vendors who manufacture those devices, is another important role a security advisor performs. It is important to understand security on how it was implemented so far in the shop floor and how, in the new world of IoT, security will be taken care of.

As an example, in one of the case studies for a large manufacturing company, there were several security vulnerabilities in legacy devices which further amplified security concerns if they are to be connected to the IoT Gateway. This is because the IoT Gateway connects to the Internet, and there are chances that hackers can target IoT devices using the Gateway. The security advisor disagreed for these devices to be used in a as it is version and recommended new devices to be procured to continue development. We brought new devices from Particle IO which is a widely used Internet of Things company that has released the powerful and secured IoT devices with built-in cellular connectivity. In addition to the device security, a security advisor is also responsible for validating security postures of Smart IoT Gateways as well as IoT Cloud Platforms.

Product Development Teams

The IoT product development team constitutes of the DevSecOps team which is a team of application developers, application security experts, and the operations team.

DevOps is an approach to software development that accelerates the build life cycle (formerly known as release engineering) using automation. DevOps focuses on continuous integration and continuous delivery of software by leveraging on-demand IT resources (infrastructure as code) and by automating the integration, test, and deployment of code. This merging of software development (Dev) and IT operations (Ops) reduces time to deployment, decreases time to market, minimizes defects, and shortens the time required to resolve issues. By introducing security controls as part of the DevOps cycle, enterprises can achieve speed of development with increased security, and such a practice is called DevSecOps.

Using DevSecOps, leading companies have been able to reduce their product release cycle time from months to (literally) days. This has enabled them to grow and lead in fast-paced, emerging markets, and IoT is one area where DevSecOps brings in a lot of value. Companies like Google, Amazon, and many others now release software many times per day. By improving the quality and cycle time of product releases and with the introduction of security in DevOps, DevSecOps has gained in popularity and been a great success for a number of enterprises in IoT product development. Traditionally, what happens in the legacy world is that developers create their code and pass it to quality assurance or testing teams, who then test the code, identify any bugs, and pass it back to developers. Developers will then fix the code and return it for more testing, before it is handed over to the operations teams for support and maintenance of the product. This is a common practice which is followed in a waterfall development methodology. An agile software development process also partly follows this model with an exception that developers and testers within the development cycle work in tandem without any handoffs, although handoffs are still passed to the operations team after testing for deployment. This clearly shows a lack of collaboration between development, testing, and deployment teams, which ultimately leads to a slow development and deployment cycle. DevSecOps eliminates this challenge completely since there is only one team for development, security, and operations, and therefore there are no handoffs.

The "always-on" nature of the Internet of Things means that organizations can continuously update software in a secured way based on feedback from connected devices using DevSecOps. On a daily basis, individuals use connected vehicles and robotics; enterprises are deploying connected factories and using IoT in their shop floors. If there is a feedback from the connected devices, the ability to address the feedback is quite easy in a DevSecOps environment. This means enterprises can fix things as they come along.

DevSecOps Enables Faster Delivery Time

The main principles of DevOps are automation, continuous delivery, and quick feedback cycle, which aim to make an IoT product development process faster, secure, and more efficient. Being an evolutionary stretch of the Agile methodology, DevSecOps utilizes automation to ensure a smooth flow of the product development process. By promoting a collaborative culture, it offers the scope for quick and continuous feedback so that any glitches are fixed in time, and the releases are done faster.

DevSecOps Manages the Scale and Is Proactively Secure

For IoT use cases, it is necessary to secure information coming in from devices and appliances, to prevent it from getting compromised. All IoT systems must patch up software vulnerabilities in a few minutes and be proactively secure. In addition, they should quickly scale from a couple of devices (during the pilot stage) to thousands of devices (production stage) in a matter of weeks; so systems should be designed to manage this load. Once DevSecOps is enabled in enterprises for their IoT use cases, the setup can scale to any number of use cases and devices. In addition, IoT

DevSecOps helps developers, testers and QA, and the IoT operation teams by automating release, vulnerability, and patch management in real time and installing patches and updates without disrupting user experience.

Manage Rigorous Interoperability Testing and Ensure Availability

IoT applications can have multiple software and hardware configurations within solutions. Testing the security, performance, connectivity, and a number of parameters for millions of devices is not an easy task. These different configurations and attributes need to be tested before deploying to production. Automated testing methodologies adopted as part of DevSecOps implementations ensure that QA processes have considerable test coverage across these different configurations and attributes.

Information Technology Lead

The IT lead is the one who comes from the IT organization. The IT lead in an IoT context is the one who not only is conversant with the IT systems but can clearly understand the nuances of OT systems that are part of the IoT use case. The IT lead needs to work alongside the OT leads and should be able to define a technology road map for IT and OT integration. This role needs to have a complete handle on IT compliance, governance, security, data center or cloud requirements, types of IT systems used within an enterprise, their integrations, and so on.

Another important capability that an Information Technology lead needs to possess is an understanding of the end-to-end IoT Standards Reference Model. They should be able to help the enterprise in shortlisting and selecting the Smart IoT Gateway and IoT Cloud platform, apart from defining the end-to-end development platform including the DevSecOps pipeline and so on. In the majority of the cases, the Information Technology lead brings in a team of senior architects to achieve the desired goals from their role.

Big Data Lead

The big data lead is one of the most important roles in an IoT implementation. IoT use cases can be successful only if data from devices or OT systems are captured, filtered, and analyzed in a way that can provide useful insights for enterprises to make decisions. Big data leads therefore form part of the core team for IoT implementation, who along with IT leads decide where data management and analytics need to happen for specific use cases, based on which Smart IoT Gateway and IoT Cloud Platform are selected.

The data lead is the one who brings in expertise to define the big data storage requirements and how data needs to be stored and governed. The big data lead also forms the data science team to enable enterprises with the insights based on the data gathered from IoT devices.

Definition

Industrial control system (ICS) **is a general term that encompasses several types of** *control systems* **and associated** *instrumentation* **used for** *industrial process control.*

Such systems can range in size from a few modular panel-mounted controllers to large interconnected and interactive distributed control systems with thousands of field connections.

IoT Champion

The IoT champion is the product director to achieve enterprise vision on IoT. This is an individual who is able to communicate with and relate to both IT and OT groups. The IT-OT integration champion understands how to convey information in a way that encourages cooperation and collaboration between all the parties involved in the integration, including

OT leads and shop floor staff. It is an important role which is about defining and redefining the goals and success criteria of OT departments to foster collaboration. The challenge is that IT and OT have different goals, philosophies, and working cultures. The IT-OT integration champion is the one who brings all these goals and people together to achieve a common objective of IT-OT integration success.

IoT Product Team Identification

Until now, we discussed about different roles that need to be part of the product team for IoT implementation. In this section, we are going to discuss about identifying a high-performing IoT team.

A high-performing team delivers exceptional results time and time again, irrespective of the challenges they encounter. We will discuss about creating a high-performing IoT team with a framework that attracts individuals who are of the right caliber to support an enterprise in their digital transformation journey using IoT.

Traditionally, enterprises follow a triangle pyramid as depicted in Figure 13-2 where juniors are placed at the bottom of the pyramid and seniors at the top. This is how traditional enterprises have operated, and it was indeed the right model since technology was stable with little unknowns. Project execution was quite methodical in nature with little to medium level of automation in project life cycles.

Referring to Figure 13-2, section C consists of resources with fewer than three years of experience and typically also includes a percentage of recent college graduates. This is called the *bottom* of the pyramid. These are typically junior developers and testers.

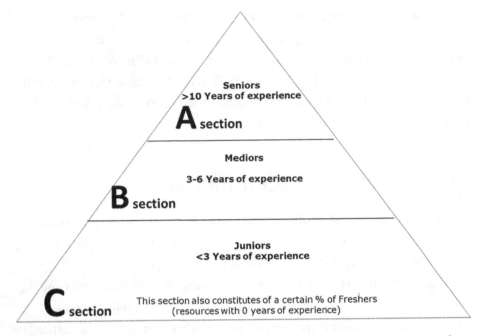

Figure 13-2. *A typical pyramid for project execution consisting of resources with different experience levels*

Section B consists of resources with mid-level experience (three to six years), also known as mediors. These are typically IoT developers and testers along with some junior designers, senior developers, and senior testers. This is also referred to as the *bottom +1* of the pyramid.

Section A consists of highly experienced technical, functional, and managerial resources, including product directors, enterprise architects, Operational Technology leads, senior designers, and senior developers and testers. This section is typically referred to as the *top –1* of the pyramid. Section A also consists of a scrum master and product manager, including enterprise and business architects, referred to as the *top* of the pyramid.

Over time, this pyramid structure has rooted into the competency of resources within an enterprise. As depicted in Figure 13-3, this means that a small portion of high-performing individuals exist within a team, and these are the ones depicted at the top of the pyramid.

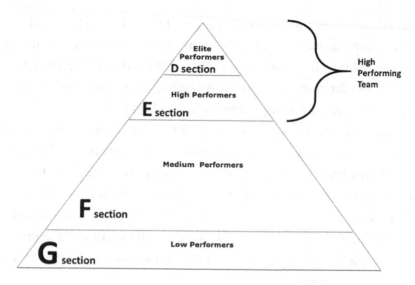

Figure 13-3. *A typical pyramid with competency levels*

Section D consists of elite performers who are the core for the success of any enterprise or engagement. These are individuals who are good at what they do and can go the extra mile to learn and adapt to any new changes within the industry or enterprise, be it from a technological or business side. They have a high appetite to learn and contribute to the overall product and enterprise success.

Section E consists of resources who are high performers and are important to the product team. These are individuals who are good at what they do and support the enterprise in their area of expertise and contribute to the overall product success.

Section F consists of resources with medium competency. These are individuals who are good at what they do but do not necessarily go the extra mile to support the program or project, not because they are not willing to but because they do not have the technical competency to do so.

Section G consists of resources who are low performers. Though many organizations will disagree with this statement, it is a well-known fact that almost all enterprises during their annual appraisal or performance review cycle fire employees in Section G from the organization.

Several enterprises are still operating in the traditional pyramid structure described earlier and at the same time are aspiring to transform their whole organization and make profits. The traditional pyramid is not the right model for enterprises that are aspiring to succeed in their digital transformation journey using technologies such as IoT.

It is essential that enterprises change their structures to ensure success in their IoT journey. A product organization need to move to a diamond structure in contrast to the traditional pyramid. Enterprises also need to move away from measuring competency of resources based on their experience level. The only measure in a diamond-based structure is the competency of individuals, which are categorized into one of the three quadrants as depicted in Figure 13-4. There is no place for low performers in a diamond structure.

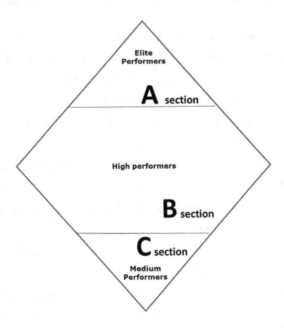

Figure 13-4. *Diamond structure with competency levels*

Section A consists of elite performers. Section B consists of competent and high-performing resources, and Section C has resources with medium competency.

Across the diamond structure in all the three sections, individuals with all variety of roles can be found, such as agile coaches, a scrum master, product managers, enterprise and business architects, and product engineering teams.

The Cost Implications of a Traditional Pyramid

In a traditional triangle pyramid, juniors fall at the bottom which constitute 50%–60% of the team, mediors fall in the middle quadrant which constitute 30%–40% of the team, and the rest are seniors which constitute roughly 10% of the team.

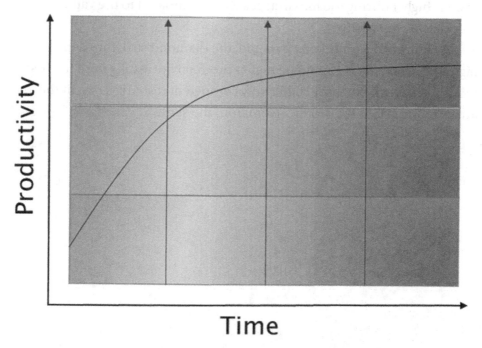

Figure 13-5. *Productivity levels for a traditional pyramid*

This model has existed for decades, and typically organizations start at a low-cost baseline since it is considered as a highly optimized pyramid. Due to the large number of juniors in this mix, the initial level productivity during the first few months is always low since the learning curve tends to be high. In addition, during my 20+ years of experience, I have seen that a minimum of roughly 20%–30% of the team gets replaced in the first six months due to a mismatch of individual competencies against project demands. Due to this, I personally have found that it takes somewhere between three and five months for a team of 20–30 resources to stabilize and deliver a reasonable level of productivity.

Figure 13-5 provides a view on how productivity levels increase and stabilize over a period of time within a traditional pyramid structure. It is clear from Figure 13-5 that the initial productivity levels are quite low and mature gradually to a stable state. This implies that the cost of the product team is higher during the initial stages when compared to the value or productivity they deliver.

In contrast to a traditional pyramid, the diamond structure depicted in Figure 13-6 provides guaranteed higher productivity results from the first month. This is due to the fact that only competent resources that fit the job are introduced into the product team from the start.

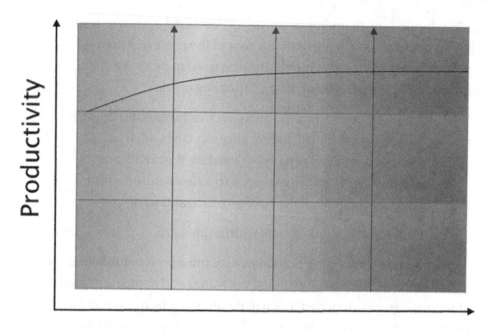

Figure 13-6. *Productivity levels of a diamond structure*

In summary, the cost of the diamond structure will not be higher than a traditional triangle pyramid once enterprises start measuring the productivity of the team over time.

My personal experience with more than six enterprises that have transitioned from a traditional pyramid to a diamond structure has demonstrated that using a diamond structure is over 30% cheaper than a traditional pyramid. This data was measured for a 12-month period in these case studies.

By adopting the diamond structure as described earlier, enterprises will reap better results in terms of the cost of the average resource compared to a traditional pyramid. Results need to be measured for a minimum of 12 months period in the following areas:

- Ramp-up costs – Any new resource inducted into the product team will incur ramp-up costs, such as increased wages compared to existing resources, cost of transition from an old resource to a new resource, time taken to understand the new product, and so on.

- Productivity of individuals within the team.

The diamond structure is mandatory for enterprises embarking on their IoT journey. It is essential that a motivated and competent product engineering team is identified that will develop the best product for an enterprise in the most agile and cost-effective manner. The Hackfest model assists in identifying the right product engineering teams, which will be discussed in more detail in the following.

Hackfest Model to Identify Product Development Teams

Hackfest is a model which provides an approach on how IoT product development teams need to be identified. Hackfest follows a step-by-step approach starting from shortlisting individuals for the product organization to the identification of competent resources until the time they are trained and deployed into individual product development teams.

The Hackfest model evaluation and selection process moves away from subjective-based evaluation to being fully objective based. Therefore, the chances of recruiting a motivated and skilled resource double compared to traditional hiring processes.

The four phases of the Hackfest model are depicted in Figure 13-7.

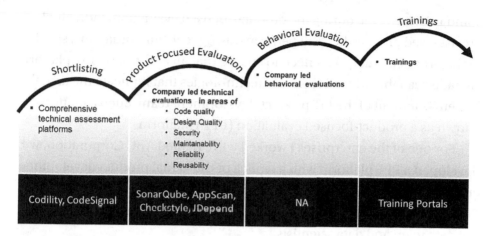

Figure 13-7. *Four phases of the Hackfest model*

Each enterprise needs to tailor the Hackfest model based on their organizational landscape following the guideline as described in the following.

Shortlisting

The first phase is the shortlisting phase, where all potential individuals of the IoT product team are evaluated comprehensively on their core skills. Enterprises need to be prepared with a technical assessment kit that can support the shortlisting of individuals for the next phase. Alternatively, there are a lot of industry-leading platforms such as Codility, CodeSignal, and HackerRank that can help enterprises in the shortlisting of resources through online coding tests specific to IoT.

Product-Focused Evaluation

The second phase is the product-focused evaluation where individuals are evaluated on their technical skills by asking them to develop proofs of concepts that are specific to the actual IoT use case. During the shortlisting phase, individuals are assessed on their core skills based on industry standards; however, during the product-focused evaluation, individuals are assessed on how they will perform during real-time situations, specific to the product. Enterprises need to ensure that an end-to-end IoT platform is made available with all tools and technologies that replicate the actual live environment of the IoT product development team. Such a platform is known as a product-focused evaluation (PFE) platform.

For one of the enterprises I worked with, named ABC Corporation, we developed a PFE platform with a replica of the actual product development environment where devices were connected to the IoT Gateway and IoT Platform. A full-fledged data platform was also made available to evaluate the data team and data scientists.

It is recommended that a PFE platform is created replicating the actual environment on which the product team will be working. Such a platform will aid in evaluating how well individuals will deliver productivity once they are deployed into the product team. Individuals need to perform development for the IoT use cases utilizing the complete PFE platform. Once development is completed by individuals, an evaluation is performed on

- Code quality

- Design quality

- Level of security considered in the code

- How well code has been written from a maintainability perspective

- How well code has been written from a reliability perspective and so on

- Reports/insights generated for the IoT use case

There are several tools available in the market which can perform the preceding validation. In the preceding case study for ABC Corporation, tools such as SonarQube were used for static code quality analysis; jDepend was used to validate design quality with respect to maintainability, performance, and reliability; and AppScan was used for code security.

Behavioral Evaluation

All applicants who successfully complete a product-focused evaluation are further assessed on their behavioral skills. Behavioral evaluation is a process to discover how interviewees act in specific employment-related situations. The logic on how one behaved in the past will likely predict how that individual will behave in the future, that is, past performance predicts future performance. There are several tools available in the market such as the Chally Assessment which assesses individuals on their behavioral skills that can be utilized, or specific in-house evaluation mechanisms can be created by enterprises themselves.

Trainings

Once an individual successfully completes the behavioral evaluation, the next step in the Hackfest model is to prepare individuals for deployment to the product team. To ensure that there is the right level of productivity achieved from day one, individuals need to be supported with training on their supporting skills, if required. Individuals should be trained to a level that they will be able to utilize the supporting skill with minimal supervision required from their superiors and peers.

Core skills are those which the job or task cannot be carried out without having.

A supporting skill is a variant of a core skill. It means that an individual will need to have this as a mandatory skill; however, they can be a beginner level in this skill, and this skill can be acquired with training or on-the-job learning. As an example, in the context of a Java developer, core skills are Java and J2EE. Supporting skills can be an experience in the C++ programming language, knowledge in a specific security tool, expertise on an operating system on cloud infrastructure, installing a tool on cloud infrastructure, monitoring infrastructure, and so on. Every product team should define core skills and supporting skills specific to the product requirement, and only individuals who possess these skills should be inducted into the product engineering team.

The Hackfest model may look like a lengthy four-stage interview process, but if you understood the nuances of this model, there is just one round of comprehensive evaluation in each area. With such an evaluation, a 360-degree assessment can be performed on each individual. As an example, with product-focused evaluations an individual is assessed on their development skills from several angles, such as code quality, security, reliability, and maintainability. This clearly articulates the coding style of an individual and provides a view on their strengths and weaknesses, based on which decisions can be made. This implies that projects will be far more successful if the right resources can be introduced in the product development teams.

With the Hackfest model, enterprises can assess hundreds of resources in one go, providing necessary infrastructure such as a PFE platform is available at scale. My own personal experience has demonstrated that a well-planned Hackfest can be completed in two days for around 200 applicants, which is quite an attractive prospect for large-scale resource requirements with tight deadlines to meet.

Summary

In this chapter, we discussed the key roles required for an IoT product team, which are listed as follows:

1. IoT champion Who leads the complete IoT program

2. Operational Technology lead – Who can bring the shop floor expertise

3. Security advisor – Across IT and OT systems

4. Product development team – Constitutes of the DevSecOps team which is a team of application developers, application security experts, and the operations team

5. Information Technology lead – Who is conversant with the IT systems and also understands the nuances of OT systems

6. Big data lead – Who sets up and chooses the data platform

As we now understand the key roles that need to be part of the product team for IoT implementation, the next step is to identify a high-performing IoT team. We discussed that enterprises need to follow a diamond structure in contrast to a traditional triangle pyramid and subsequently use the Hackfest model to identify product teams. The Hackfest model has four phases, namely, the shortlisting phase, product-focused evaluation phase, behavioral evaluation phase, and the training phase. With the Hackfest model, enterprises move away from subjective-based evaluation process to fully objective based.

Following the principles and models laid out in this chapter, any enterprises will be able to create a high-performing product team.

Summary of the Book

Overall, this book is about business-driven digital transformation using IoT. A business-driven digital transformation means that business goals define the technology road map and not vice versa. The Internet of Things (IoT) is one such technology that enables digital transformation for enterprises.

The Internet of Things (IoT) is all about connecting devices and factory equipment over the Internet to derive insights that enterprises can use to become competitive in the market or do operations in a highly optimized and cost-effective way.

In the first part of this book, we introduced readers to the generic industry perspective on digital transformation using IoT. We also discussed about the three business strategies for enterprises to adopt and remain relevant in the marketspace – the Customer Engagement Strategy, the Business Transformation Strategy, and the Business Productivity Improvement Strategy. It is necessary that enterprises choose a business strategy to ensure that a clear mission and vision is established based on which IoT road map can be defined. Subsequently, all business processes pertaining to the chosen business strategy are investigated to define use cases where IoT can be adopted to achieve the business strategy.

In the second part, we discussed about the IoT Standards Reference Model which is an abstract framework consisting of an interlinked set of clearly defined components, using which enterprises can successfully implement an IoT solution. The IoT Standards Reference Model can be applied for IoT use cases across any industries and is kept abstract in order to enable many, potentially different, IoT architectures to be implemented based on the IoT Standards Reference model.

In this part, we also discussed about the challenges faced by enterprises while implementing IoT use cases and how to overcome those using the IoT Standards Reference Model. The challenges range from device diversity and their communication protocols to the IoT Gateways that connect these IoT devices together followed by the IoT Cloud Platform that enterprises use for storing big data and performing analytics.

The third part of the book discussed about the importance of Artificial Intelligence and Blockchain for IoT use cases.

Blockchain is one of the interesting topics in the technology circles, which is currently revolutionizing the way enterprises will do business in the future. We discussed the importance of using private blockchain for IoT use cases along with the five IoT-Blockchain implementation patterns, using which enterprises can enable seamless communication between IoT devices, Smart IoT Gateways, and IoT platforms to blockchain. These patterns will help achieve trust, interoperability, and extendibility, which is one of the major challenges faced by enterprises in IoT implementation today.

Artificial Intelligence (AI) is the next topic and is the art of making machines smart by teaching them to be like humans. Artificial Intelligence is one of the very important features within the IoT Standards Reference Model. The reference model recommends applying AI patterns to generate insights from data and take appropriate actions automatically. A perspective on how and when to apply AI in an IoT context is also provided.

In the final part of the book, we discussed about the execution aspects of IoT, centered around big data and analytics, product organization, and the IoT product team.

With IoT at the helm of digital transformation, the complexity of managing data has increased several folds because until now we are talking about terabytes and petabytes of data, and with IoT we will be dealing with zettabytes of data. In this part, we discussed how to set up an efficient data platform using the Data First Reference Model that will enable enterprises to spend less money and efforts toward managing their data platform and focus more on actual insights and actions. We also discussed about the key capabilities that enterprises need to validate from a data perspective, based on which they can choose the right products for their IoT use cases.

Subsequently, we also discussed about product organization to implement IoT use cases. It is very essential for enterprises to move from a project-based thinking to a product organization to reap the benefits from IoT use cases. However, this is a very complex transformation and involves a massive shift to the human resource function of an enterprise. In this part, we discussed about how enterprises can transform themselves to a product-based organization and how a human resource function within an enterprise needs to change. Finally, in this part, we discussed about the IoT product team that will be responsible for making IoT use case implementation successful. We discussed about the different roles required for IoT implementation and how IT and OT teams need to come together to make IoT use cases successful.

Overall, this book defined an enterprise digital transformation framework for IoT, called IoT Standards, that will enable enterprises to do business better and achieve operational benefits using IoT.

Index

A

AAEON gateways, 119

Active data source, 216

Active monitoring, 5

Advanced driver assistance systems (ADAS), 92

Agile software development methodology

BDUF approach, 234

benefits, 235

communication/collaboration, 237

continuous learning/developments, 236

cost control, 237

De Facto methodology, 235

definition, 234

development methodology, 234

failing late, 237

flexibility, 236

frequent value delivered, 236

higher team morale, 238

high-quality, 238

life cycle models, 233

traditional software, 234

transparency, 237

Amazon Web Services (AWS), 36, 126

Application enablement platforms, 136–137

Application program / programming interface (API), security, 154–156

Artificial Intelligence (AI), 64, 74

cognitive computing, 189

computer vision, 189

data perspective, 193

data science, 190–193

deep learning algorithms, 188

definition, 187

digital transformation, 263

digital transformation/automation, 183

IoT platform

amplifying benefits, 193

data and time learning, 196

data perspective, 193

model working process, 197

narrow task performances, 196

NASA, 192

predefined rule, 192

predictions, 194

proof of concept, 195

scalability/agility, 193